Maths

Assessment Papers
Up to Speed

9-10 years

Great Clarendon Street, Oxford, OX2 6DP, United Kingdom

Oxford University Press is a department of the University of Oxford. It furthers the University's objective of excellence in research, scholarship, and education by publishing worldwide. Oxford is a registered trade mark of Oxford University Press in the UK and in certain other countries

Text © Paul Broadbent 2015
Illustrations © Oxford University Press 2015

The moral rights of the authors have been asserted

First published in 2015
This edition published in 2022

All rights reserved. No part of this publication may be reproduced, stored in a retrieval system, or transmitted, in any form or by any means, without the prior permission in writing of Oxford University Press, or as expressly permitted by law, by licence or under terms agreed with the appropriate reprographics rights organization. Enquiries concerning reproduction outside the scope of the above should be sent to the Rights Department, Oxford University Press, at the address above.

You must not circulate this work in any other form and you must impose this same condition on any acquirer

British Library Cataloguing in Publication Data
Data available

978-0-19-278509-1

10 9 8 7 6 5

Paper used in the production of this book is a natural, recyclable product made from wood grown in sustainable forests.
The manufacturing process conforms to the environmental regulations of the country of origin.

Printed in Great Britain by Ashford Colour Ltd.

Acknowledgements

The publishers would like to thank the following for permissions to use copyright material:

Page make-up: GreenGate Publishing Services, Tonbridge, Kent
Cover illustrations: Lo Cole

Although we have made every effort to trace and contact all copyright holders before publication this has not been possible in all cases. If notified, the publisher will rectify any errors or omissions at the earliest opportunity.

Links to third party websites are provided by Oxford in good faith and for information only. Oxford disclaims any responsibility for the materials contained in any third party website referenced in this work.

The manufacturer's authorised representative in the EU for product safety is Oxford University Press España S.A. of El Parque Empresarial San Fernando de Henares, Avenida de Castilla, 2 – 28830 Madrid (www.oup.es/en or product.safety@oup.com). OUP España S.A. also acts as importer into Spain of products made by the manufacturer.

Introduction

What is Bond?

The Bond *Up to Speed* titles are part of the Bond range of assessment papers, the number one series for the 11+, selective exams and general practice. Bond *Up to Speed* is carefully designed to support children who need less challenging activities than those in the regular age-appropriate Bond papers, in order to build up and improve their techniques and confidence.

How does this book work?

The book contains two distinct sets of papers, along with full answers and a Progress Chart:

- Focus tests, accompanied by advice and directions, are focused on particular (and age-appropriate) Maths question types encountered in the 11+ and other exams. The questions are deliberately set at a less challenging level than the standard *Assessment Papers*. Each Focus test is designed to help a child 'catch' their level in a particular question type, and then gently raise it through the course of the test and the subsequent Mixed papers.

- Mixed papers are longer tests containing a full range of Maths question types. These are designed to provide rigorous practice with less challenging questions, perhaps against the clock, in order to help children acquire and develop the necessary skills and techniques for 11+ success.

Full answers are provided for both types of test in the middle of the book.

Some questions may require a ruler or protractor. Calculators are not permitted.

How much time should the tests take?

The tests are for practice and to reinforce learning, and you may wish to test exam techniques and working to a set time limit. Using the Mixed papers, we would recommend that your child spends 60 minutes answering the 50 questions in each paper.

You can reduce the suggested time by 5 minutes to practise working at speed.

Using the Progress Chart

The Progress Chart can be used to track Focus test and Mixed paper results over time to monitor how well your child is doing and identify any repeated problems in tackling the different question types.

Focus test 1 — Place value

Look at the value of each digit in a number:

41 735

40 000 + 1000 + 700 + 30 + 5

forty-one thousand seven hundred and thirty-five

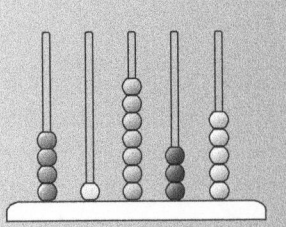

1 Write the number at each arrow on this number line.

2 Write these numbers in order of size, starting with the smallest.

6412   6900
4395   4953

____ ____ ____ ____

Smallest →

3 Round 4755 m to the nearest 100 m. ____ m

Read these and write each as a number.

4 thirty-four thousand four hundred and twelve ____

5 sixteen thousand and eight ____

6 Write the number that is 100 more than 67 052. ____

Decimal numbers are any numbers made from the digits 0 to 9.
A decimal point is used to separate whole numbers from decimals.

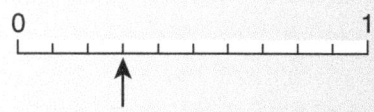

This shows tenths.

0.3 is the same as $\frac{3}{10}$

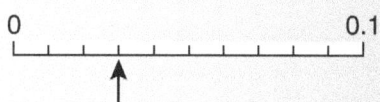

This shows hundredths.

0.03 is the same as $\frac{3}{100}$

Circle the number that is the same value as each fraction.

7 $\frac{7}{10}$ 70   7   0.7   0.07

8 $\frac{9}{100}$ 900   90   0.9   0.09

9 Write < or > to make this number sentence true.

10.16 _____ 10.9

10 Write this set of decimals in order, starting with the smallest.

9.36   **39.6**   **9.63**   **6.39**

_____ < _____ < _____ < _____

11 Round 3.56 kg to the nearest tenth. _____ kg

12 Complete these calculations.

62 ÷ 10 = _____

0.07 × 10 = _____

Now go to the Progress Chart to record your score!   Total   12

Focus test 2 — Addition and subtraction

Write the missing numbers to complete these additions.

1)
```
   5 6 3 ☐
+  2 ☐ 4 6
─────────
   8 2 ☐ 8
```

2)
```
   4 ☐ 4 8
+  3 9 0 ☐
─────────
   8 5 ☐ 2
```

> When you add decimals, remember to line up the decimal points. The method is the same as with whole numbers.
>
> *Example*
>
> What is the total of 12.6, 3.5 and 2.93?
>
> ```
>     1 2 . 6
>       3 . 5
> +     2 . 9 3
> ───────────
>     1 9 . 0 3
> ```

Complete these additions.

3)
```
      7.3
    1 3.9
+     8.5
────────
```

4)
```
    5 7.2
      6.2
+   4 3.8
────────
```

5) Write the total weight for this group of parcels. _____ kg

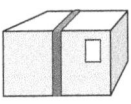 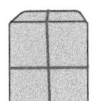

25.9 kg   23.7 kg   9.65 kg

Complete these calculations.

6)
```
    9 3 0 6
  − 6 0 2 8
──────────
```

7)
```
    7 1 9 4
  − 3 8 7 7
──────────
```

8 Joel bought a tennis racket for £32.65 and a tube of tennis balls for £6.80.

How much did he spend in total? £_____

How much change did he get from £50? £_____

Try using a number line to count on to find the difference between numbers.

Example

What is the difference between 17.8 and 26?

Draw a blank number line from 17.8 to 26. Count on to 18, then on to 26 to find the difference:

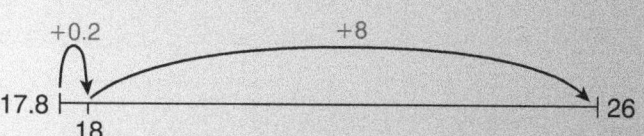

The difference is 8.2.

---

9 Find the difference between each pair of numbers.

26.7 ├──────────────┤ 45   _____

19.6 ├──────────────┤ 32   _____

10 Write the missing numbers on this difference grid.

−	2.5	3.1	6.7
1.4	1.1	___	___
5.6	___	2.5	___
7.3	___	___	___

Look at these numbers.

13.7   21.8   19.6   27.3

11 What is the difference between the largest and smallest number? _____

12 Which two numbers have a difference of 2.2? _____ and _____

Focus test 3 — Multiplication and division

Try to learn all your tables facts. These are the facts that probably cause the most problems, so practise these until you know them:

9 × 6   4 × 7   6 × 7   3 × 8   4 × 8
6 × 8   7 × 8   4 × 9   7 × 9   8 × 9

1 This is a 'multiply by 4' machine.
   Write the missing numbers in the chart.

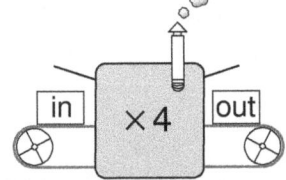

IN	3	8	___	10	___	4
OUT	12	___	28	___	24	___

2 There are six pencils in a box. How many pencils are there in eight boxes? ___

3 There are seven days in a week. How many days are there in nine weeks? ___

4 Write =, < or > to make each statement true.

   18 ÷ 2 ___ 9   7 × 6 ___ 50   56 ÷ 7 ___ 6

With a grid method for multiplication, multiply each pair of numbers to complete the grid. Then add the numbers to find the total.

Example: What is 16 multiplied by 4?

×	10	6
4	40	24	→ 64

5 Use this grid to multiply 18 by 7.

×	10	8
7			→ _____

6 What is 48 multiplied by 3? _____

7 Here are some number cards.

Use two of these cards as digits to make a number that can be divided exactly by 9.

_____ _____

8 Tennis balls are sold in tubes of 4. How many balls will there be in 65 tubes? _____

9 A box holds 6 tins of dog food. How many boxes are needed for 48 tins? _____

If a number cannot be divided exactly it leaves a remainder.

What is 85 divided by 4 and what is the remainder?

```
    2 1  r 1              85 ÷ 4 = 21 remainder 1
 4) 8 5
  - 8 0   (4 × 20)
    ---
      5
    - 4   (4 × 1)
    ---
      1
```

Complete these calculations.

10 5) 6 7   11 3) 5 8   12 4) 9 5

Now go to the Progress Chart to record your score!   Total ◯ 12

Focus test 4 — Factors, multiples and prime numbers

> Factors are those numbers that will divide exactly into other numbers. Factors of numbers can be put into pairs:
>
> Factors of 15 → (1, 15) (3, 5)   15 has four factors.
>
> Factors of 18 → (1, 18) (2, 9) (3, 6)   18 has six factors.

1 Write the missing factors of 24.

   24 → (1, 24) (2, ____) (3, ____) (____, ____)

2 Circle the numbers that are factors of 12.

   1   2   3   4   5   6   7   8   9   10   11   12

3 Write the factors of 49 in order, starting with the smallest.

   ____, ____, ____

> A prime number only has two factors, 1 and itself. For example, 7 is a prime number as it can only be divided exactly by 1 and 7. The number 1 is not a prime number.

4 What are the first four prime numbers? ____ ____ ____ ____

5 After the number 2, every prime number is an odd number.

   True or False? _____

> A multiple is a number made by multiplying together two other numbers. For example, the multiples of 5 are 5, 10, 15, 20, and so on.

6 Circle the numbers that are multiples of both 2 and 3.

   12   15   6   9   10   18   24

7 Write each of these numbers in the correct place on the Venn diagram.

30   25   18   16

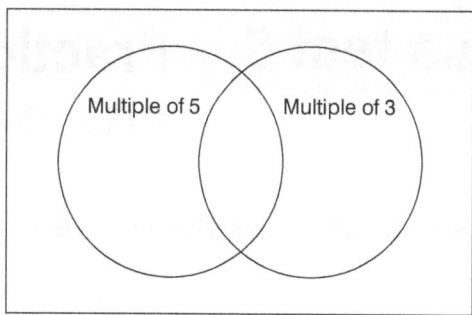

8 I am thinking of a number. It is a multiple of 4 and a multiple of 7. It is between 50 and 60. What is the number I am thinking of? _____

9 Circle all the multiples of 3 and underline all the factors of 15.

8   10   15   9   5   3   30

10 Write each number in the correct place on this Carroll diagram.

6   8   10   16

	Multiple of 4	Not a multiple of 4
Factor of 24		
Not a factor of 24		

11 Complete these multiplications.

1 × 1 = _____

2 × 2 = _____

3 × 3 = _____

12 Complete these calculations.

4^2 = _____

5^2 = _____

6^2 = _____

A number multiplied by itself gives a square number.

3 × 3 = 9

3^2 = 9

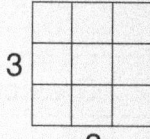

Now go to the Progress Chart to record your score!   Total   12

Focus test 5 — Fractions, decimals and percentages

Equivalent fractions have the same value, even though they may look different.

$\frac{3}{12} = \frac{1}{4}$

$\frac{3}{12}$ is simplified to $\frac{1}{4}$

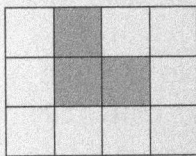

Write the fraction of each shape that is shaded. Simplify each fraction.

1   2   3

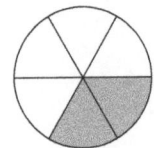 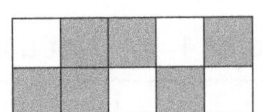 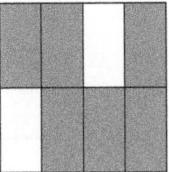

_____   _____   _____

Circle **two** fractions that have the same value as the first fraction.

4 $\frac{2}{3}$ $\frac{5}{9}$ $\frac{8}{12}$ $\frac{4}{8}$ $\frac{6}{9}$

5 $\frac{3}{10}$ $\frac{9}{20}$ $\frac{4}{15}$ $\frac{6}{20}$ $\frac{30}{100}$

6 Use ticks to complete this chart.

	Greater than $\frac{1}{2}$	Less than $\frac{1}{2}$
0.45		
0.54		

7 Draw lines to match each fraction to its equivalent decimal.

$\frac{1}{2}$ $\frac{3}{4}$ $\frac{2}{5}$ $\frac{3}{10}$ $\frac{1}{4}$ $\frac{9}{10}$

0.25   0.75   0.5   0.4   0.9   0.3

8 Circle the smallest decimal and underline the largest decimal.

0.4   0.25   0.6   0.01   0.1   0.7

To change fractions to percentages, make them out of 100. This means you need to find the equivalent fraction with the denominator 100.

Example

$\frac{3}{10}$ is equivalent to $\frac{30}{100}$ so $\frac{3}{10}$ = 30%

To change a percentage to a fraction, make it a fraction out of 100 and then simplify it.

Example

5% is $\frac{5}{100}$, which is the same as $\frac{1}{20}$.

% is the percentage sign: *per cent* means 'out of 100'.

---

9 What fraction of this rectangle is shaded? Simplify the fraction. _____

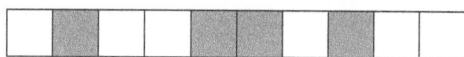

10 Circle the percentage of this rectangle that is shaded.

20%   80%   40%   75%   60%

11 Shade more of the squares so that 80% of the rectangle is shaded in total.

12 Look at these fractions.

$\frac{1}{5}$ $\frac{7}{10}$ $\frac{1}{3}$ $\frac{3}{4}$ $\frac{2}{5}$

Which fraction is equivalent to $\frac{3}{9}$? _____

Which fraction has the same value as 20%? _____

Which fraction has the same value as 0.75? _____

Now go to the Progress Chart to record your score!   Total ⬚ 12

Focus test 6 — Sequences

A sequence is a list of numbers in a pattern.

You can often find the rule for a sequence by looking at the difference between the numbers.

What is the next number in this sequence?

  35   39   43   47   ___

Each number is 4 more than the previous number, so the next number is 51.

The rule is 'add 4'.

What is the next number in each sequence?

1 54   45   36   27   ___

2 145   195   245   295   ___

3 Write the missing numbers on this grid.

1	2	3	4	5			8	9	10
20	19				15	14	13		11
21	22	23			26	27		29	
40		38		36			33		31
	42				46		48		50

Write the missing number in each sequence.

4 2.5   3.1   ___   4.3   4.9

5 3   0   ___   −6   −9

6 What are the next two numbers in this sequence?

16   31   46   61   ____   ____

7 What is the rule for this sequence?

8   5   2   −1   −4   −7

The rule is _____

8 Will −15 be in the sequence above? Yes or No? _____

Write the missing numbers in each sequence.

9 0.7   1.2   ____   2.2   2.7   ____

10 $\frac{1}{4}$ $\frac{1}{2}$ ____   1 $1\frac{1}{4}$ ____

11 What is the rule for this sequence?

1   2   4   8   16   32

The rule is _____

12 What are the next three numbers in this sequence?

150   300   450   600   ____   ____   ____

Now go to the Progress Chart to record your score!   Total   12

Focus test 7 — Shapes and angles

Here are the properties of different triangles:

Equilateral	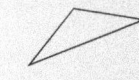 Isosceles	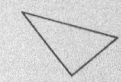 Right-angled	 Scalene
• 3 equal sides • 3 equal angles	• 2 equal sides • 2 equal angles	• one angle is a right-angle	• no equal sides • no equal angles

Name these triangles.

1 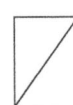   2    3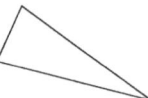

_____   _____   _____

4 An isosceles triangle can also be a right-angled triangle.
   True or False? _____

5 Cross out the shape that is **not** a quadrilateral.

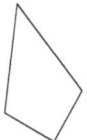 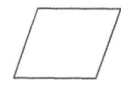  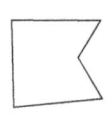 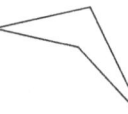

6 How many lines of symmetry are there on a regular hexagon? _____

7 Draw a symmetrical quadrilateral on this grid.
   Show the lines of symmetry with a dotted line.

3-D shapes are made up of faces, edges and vertices (corners).
This square-based pyramid has 5 faces, 8 edges, 5 vertices.

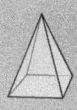

8 Complete this chart.

Name of shape	Number of faces	Number of vertices	Number of edges
Cube	___	___	___
Tetrahedron	___	___	___

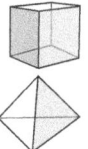

9 Write the name of each shape.

  _____   _____

10 How many faces does a cuboid have? _____

11 Look at this trapezium and complete the chart.

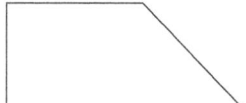

Type of angle	Acute	Obtuse	Right
Number of angles	___	___	___

A protractor is used to measure the size of an angle. It is a good idea to estimate the angle first and then measure it.

12 Measure these angles accurately with a protractor.

Angle a = _____ °

Angle b = _____ °

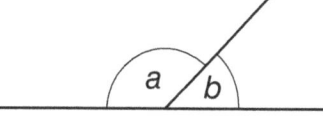

These are special types of angles to remember:

straight line	180°	⌒	acute angle	less than 90°	∠
right angle	90°	⌐	obtuse angle	between 90° and 180°	∠

Now go to the Progress Chart to record your score!   Total   12

Focus test 8 — Area and perimeter

The area of a shape is the amount of surface that it covers. You can find the area of shapes by counting squares. Area is usually measured in square centimetres or square metres, written as cm^2 and m^2. Always remember to write this at the end of the measurement.

The area of a rectangle is length × width.

Example

Area = 3 cm × 4 cm

= 12 square centimetres ($12\,cm^2$)

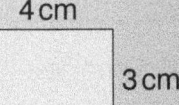

1. Draw a shape on this grid with an area of 15 squares.

2. What is the area of this shape? _____ squares

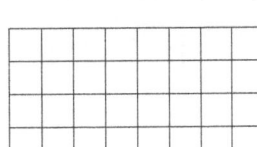

3. A rectangle has an area of 48 square centimetres. One side is 6 cm long.

   What is the length of the other side?

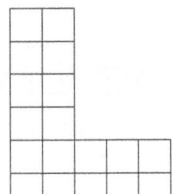

4. Calculate the area of this rectangle.

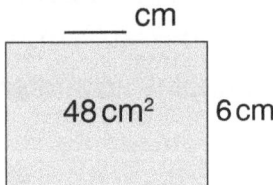

_____ cm^2

5. Draw a square on this grid with an area of $25\,cm^2$. Use a ruler.

The perimeter of a shape is the distance all the way around the edge. If the shape has straight sides, add up the lengths of all the sides. You can work out the perimeter of a rectangle by totalling the length and width and then doubling the total.

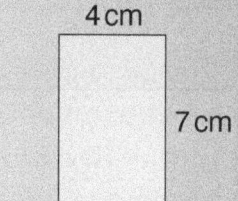

- Add together the length and width:
  7 cm + 4 cm = 11 cm
- Double 11 cm is 22 cm.
- So the perimeter of rectangle is 22 cm.

Calculate the perimeter of each rectangle.

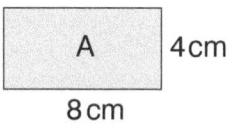
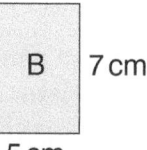

6 Perimeter of A = _____ cm

7 Perimeter of B = _____ cm

8 Which shape has the larger area, A or B? _____

What is the area and perimeter of the room shown in this diagram?

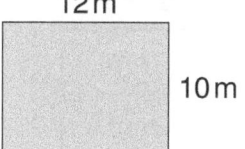

9 Area = _____ m²

10 Perimeter = _____ m

11 A square has an area of 9 cm² and a perimeter of 12 cm.

What is the length of one side of this square? _____ cm

12

Draw a line to join the two shapes with the same size area.

Tick the two shapes with the same length perimeter.

Focus test 9 — Measures

Length, weight (or mass) and capacity are all measured using different units.

Length	1 metre (m) = 100 centimetres (cm)
	1 cm = 10 millimetres (mm)
	1 kilometre (km) = 1000 m
Weight	1 kilogram (kg) = 1000 grams (g)
Capacity	1 litre (l) = 1000 millilitres (ml)

Once you know these then you can convert from one unit to another by multiplying or dividing by 10, 100 or 1000.

Examples

35 mm = 3.5 cm   2.3 kg = 2300 g   1500 ml = 1.5 litres

1. Convert each of these lengths to complete the table.

Metres	Centimetres	Millimetres
6.5 m	___ cm	___ mm
___ m	720 cm	___ mm
___ m	___ cm	3000 mm

2. How many millilitres are there in 4.8 litres? _____ ml

3. How many grams are there in 0.6 kilograms? _____ g

4. Which is heavier, $3\frac{1}{4}$ kg or 3400 g? _____

5. Write these lengths in order, starting with the shortest.

85 mm   0.8 m   85 cm   8.5 m

_____ _____ _____ _____

Shortest →

A scale is a row of marks to help us measure on a jug or ruler, for example. You need to read them accurately.

Look at the unit. Is it ml, cm, g…?

- If the level is in line with a mark, read off that number.
- If it is between numbers, work out what each mark means and count on or back.

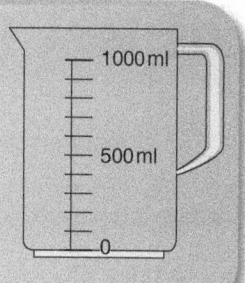

Read the scales and write how much water is in each jug.

6 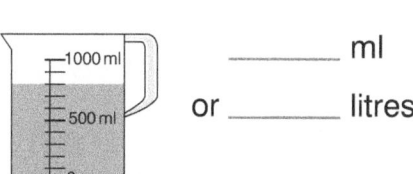 _____ ml or _____ litres

7 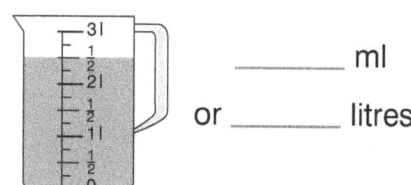 _____ ml or _____ litres

8 Measure the sides of this triangle with a ruler. Measure two sides in millimetres and the other side to the nearest half centimetre.

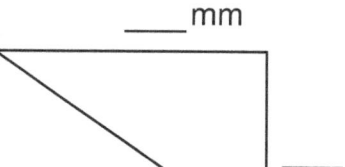

9 Draw an arrow on the scale to show 6.4 kg.

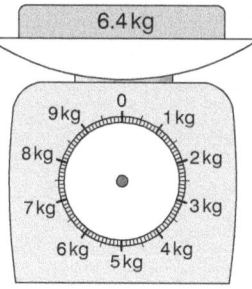

10 What is the most likely amount of water needed to fill a mug?

Circle the answer.

30 litres   3 litres

30 ml   300 ml

11 A train should arrive at 4:35 p.m but it is 20 minutes late. What time will the train actually arrive?

Write the time on the digital clock and draw the time on the clock face.

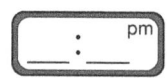 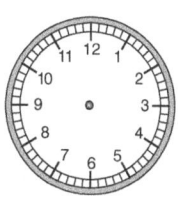

12 A film starts at 7:10 p.m and lasts for an hour and a half.

What time will the film finish? _____

Now go to the Progress Chart to record your score!   Total   12

Focus test 10 — Transformations and coordinates

Coordinates are used to show positions on a grid.

Coordinates are always pairs of numbers written in brackets and separated by a comma.

The number on the horizontal x-axis is written first, then the number on the vertical y-axis.

The coordinates of A are (−2, 4).

The coordinates of B are (5, 3).

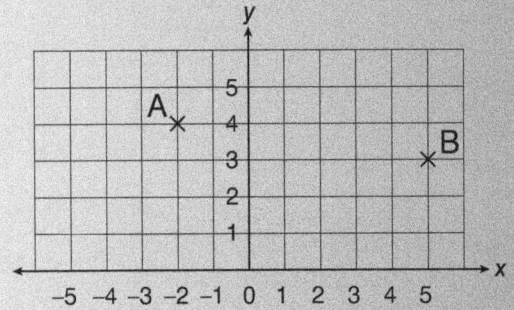

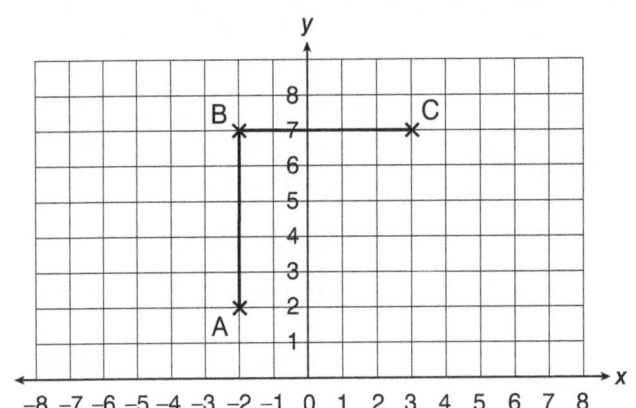

1. What are the coordinates of point A?   (____, ____)

2. What are the coordinates of point B?   (____, ____)

3. What are the coordinates of point C?   (____, ____)

4. A, B and C are three vertices of a square. Mark the missing fourth vertex with a cross and label it D. Join the vertices to make a square.

5. What are the coordinates of point D?   (____, ____)

6 Plot an isosceles triangle on this grid. Label the vertices A, B and C.

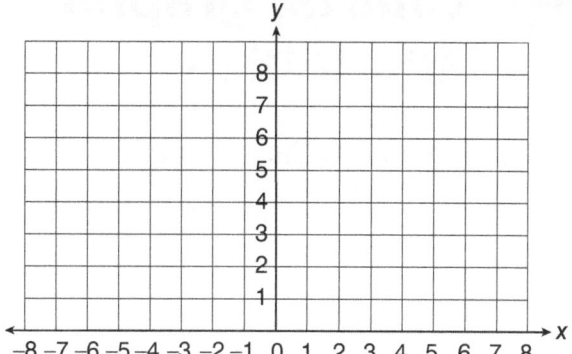

7 What are the coordinates of your triangle?

A → (____, ____)   B → (____, ____)   C → (____, ____)

A shape can be moved in three ways.
- Rotation: the shape is rotated about a point, clockwise or anticlockwise.
- Reflection: this is sometimes called 'flipping over'.
- Translation: this is sliding the shape across, up, down or diagonally, without rotating or flipping over.

Write whether these shapes have been **translated**, **rotated** or **reflected**.

8
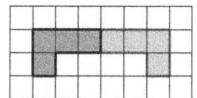
_____

9
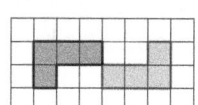
_____

10
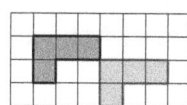
_____

This tile is used to make a pattern.

11 Has the tile been rotated, translated or reflected to make this pattern?

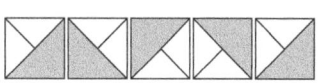

_____

12 Use the tile to make a different pattern. Have you used a translation, rotation or reflection?

_____

Focus test 11 — Charts, graphs and tables

The numbers 1–20 have been written on this Carroll diagram.

	Odd number	**Not an odd number**
Multiple of 3	3 9 15	6 12 18
Not a multiple of 3	1 5 7 11 13 17 19	2 4 8 10 14 16 20

1 Write these numbers in the correct place on the diagram.

21   22   23   24   25

Now look at the Carroll diagram with your numbers added and answer these questions.

2 How many numbers are both odd and multiples of 3? _____

3 How many numbers are not odd and not a multiple of 3? _____

4 How many numbers in total are not a multiple of 3? _____

To understand bar charts and other types of graphs, look carefully at the different parts of the graph before you look at the bars.

- Read the title. What is it about?
- Look at the axis labels. These explain the lines that go across and up.
- Work out the scale. Does it go up in 1s, 2s, 5s, 10s…?

The information from the Carroll diagram has been drawn on a block graph.

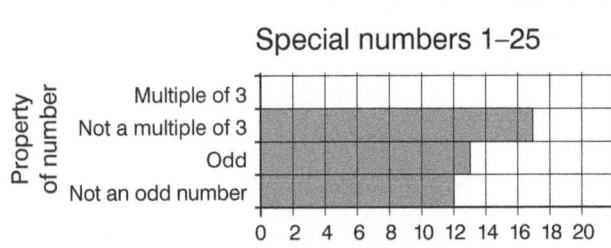

5 Count how many numbers are multiples of 3 and draw the missing block on this graph.

Use the information on the block graph to answer these questions.

6 How many numbers are even? _____

7 How many more odd numbers are there than even numbers? _____

8 How many odd and even numbers are there in total? _____

This is a conversion chart for changing litres into pints and pints into litres.

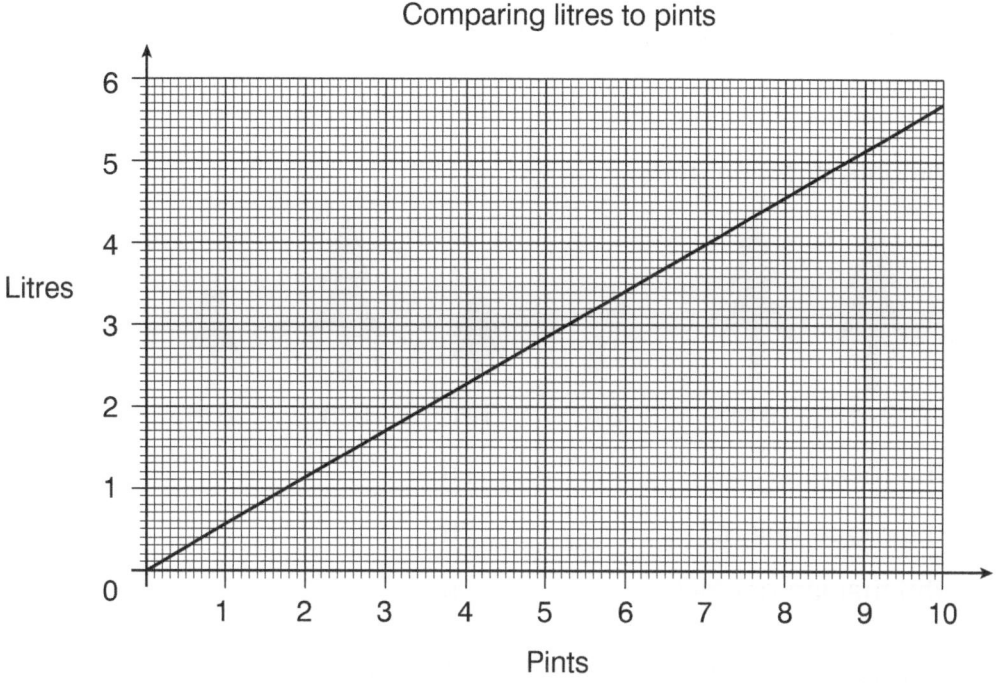

9 Approximately how many pints are the same as 4 litres? _____ pints

10 How many litres are about the same as $3\frac{1}{2}$ pints? _____ litres

11 How much is 1 pint to the nearest 100 ml? _____ ml

12 Which is greater, 5 pints or 5 litres? _____

Now go to the Progress Chart to record your score!   Total   12

Focus test 12 — Mean, median, mode and probability

- The mode of a set of data is the item that occurs the most often.
- The median is the middle number in a set of numbers when arranged in order.
- The mean of a set of numbers is their total divided by the number of items.

These are the heights of seven trees.

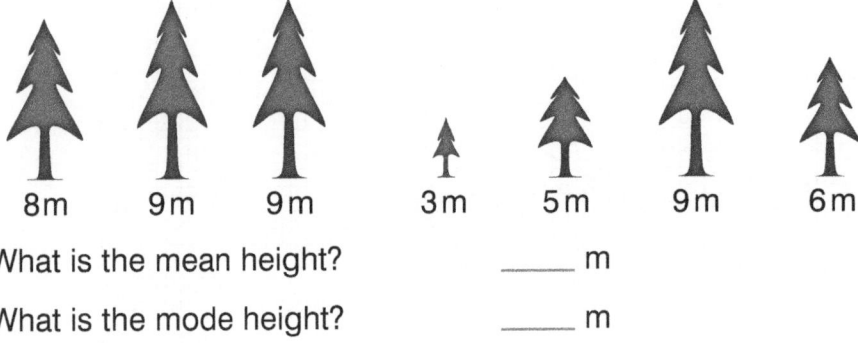

8 m   9 m   9 m   3 m   5 m   9 m   6 m

1 What is the mean height? _____ m

2 What is the mode height? _____ m

3 What is the median height? _____ m

Two trees are cut down. Draw a line through the 3 m and 6 m trees. What is the median and mean of the remaining five trees?

4 What is the new median? _____ m

5 What is the new mean? _____ m

6 What is the chance of seeing a bird today? Underline the answer.

impossible   poor chance   even chance   good chance   certain

A probability scale can be used to show how likely an event is to happen.

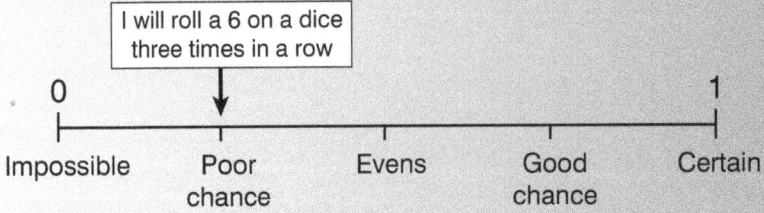

Explanations in the main text of the book are referred to *by their page*; all other questions referred to can be found in the answer section.

Focus test 1 (pages 4–5)

1 **4200, 4830** Find the difference between the numbers (5000 − 4000 = 1000) and, as the line has been separated into 10 equal parts, divide the answer by 10 (1000 ÷ 10 = 100). Therefore each large division is 100. Between each 100, the line has been separated into another 10 equal parts so each small line represents 10 (100 ÷ 10 = 10).

4000 4100 4200 4300 4400 4500 4600 4700 4800 4900 5000

2 **4395, 4953, 6412, 6900** Put the numbers in a place value grid, as shown. Look for the smallest digit in the first column. If any digits are the same, find the smallest in the next column.

Th	H	T	O
6	4	1	2
6	9	0	0
4	3	9	5
4	9	5	3

3 **4800 m** To round a number, find the digit in the place being rounded to and look at the digit to its right. If the digit to its right is 5 or more, increase the digit being rounded to by 1; if the digit to its right is 4 or less, the digit being rounded to remains the same. Here, 7 is in the hundreds place and 5 is to its right, so 7 increases by 1 and the following digits change to 0.

4–6 Insert the numbers into a place value grid to help write the answer.

TTh	Th	H	T	O
3	4	4	1	2
1	6	0	0	8
6	7	0	5	2

4 **34 412**   5 **16 008**
6 **67 152** 0 is in the hundreds place, so this digit increases by 1.
7 **0.7** In the example shown on page 5, '0.3 is the same as $\frac{3}{10}$' therefore $\frac{7}{10}$ is the same as 0.7.
8 **0.09** In the example shown on page 5, '0.03 is the same as $\frac{3}{100}$' therefore $\frac{9}{100}$ is the same as 0.09.
9 **<** < means the number on the left is less than the number on the right and > means the number on the left is greater than the number on the right. Insert the numbers into a grid ensuring the decimal points are lined up. Write 0 in any gaps after the decimal point (10.9 is the same as 10.90). Compare the digits in the first column; if any are the same, compare the digits in the next column. Both numbers begin with 1 and 0 so move to the column after the decimal point; 1 < 9 so 10.16 < 10.90

1	0	•	1	6
1	0	•	9	0

10 **6.39 < 9.36 < 9.63 < 39.6** 39 is the greatest number before the decimal point, so this will be last. Refer to Q9 on comparing decimal numbers and sort the rest of the numbers by looking for the smallest digit in each column.
11 **3.6 kg** Refer to Q3 on rounding; 5 is in the tenths place and 6 is to its right, so 5 increases by 1; as it is being rounded to tenths, the last digit will be in the tenths place.
12 **6.2, 0.7** Place the numbers in a place value grid. Move the number 1 place to the right to divide by 10 and move it 1 place to the left to multiply by 10.

	T	O	•	t	th
		6	2	•	
÷ 10			6	•	2
			0	•	0	7
× 10		0	0	•	7

Focus test 2 (pages 6–7)

1–2 Work from right to left, as when completing other column additions. Think of the equation in each column as a missing number sentence to help (e.g. ☐ + 6 = 8). Also, consider if any digits have been carried over (e.g. to find a number that ends in 2 when adding to 6: 6 + 6 = 12 so the 1 will be carried over to the next column).

```
   5 6 3 2         4 6 4 8
 + 2 6 4 6       + 3 9 0 4
   ───────         ───────
   8 2 7 8         8 5 5 2
     1             1   1
```

1 2 + 6 = 8; 3 + 4 = **7**; 6 + 6 = 12 and 1 is carried over to the next column; 5 + 2 + 1 = 8
2 8 + 4 = 12 and 1 is carried over into the next column; 4 + 0 + 1 = **5**; 6 + 9 = 15 and 1 is carried over into the next column; 4 + 3 + 1 = 8
3 **29.7**   4 **107.2**

5 **59.25 kg** If numbers have a different amount of digits after the decimal point, try inserting a 0 in any gaps at the end of the number, as shown.

```
    2  5 . 9  0
    2  3 . 7  0
+      9 . 6  5
  ─────────────
    5  9 . 2  5
       1  2
```

6 **3278** When completing column subtraction, if the digit at the top is smaller than the one below it, regroup (borrow) from the top digit in the next column. When regrouping from zero, always change it into a 9 and regroup from the digit at the top of the next column instead.

```
    9  ²3  ⁹0  ¹6
 -  6   0   2   8
   ───────────────
    3   2   7   8
```

7 **3317** Refer to Q6 on column subtraction.

```
    ⁶7  ¹1  ⁸9  ¹4
 -   3   8   7   7
    ───────────────
     3   3   1   7
```

8 **£39.45, £10.55** Refer to Q5 on adding decimal numbers (£32.65 + £6.80 = £39.45). When subtracting decimal numbers, line up the decimal points and subtract in the same way as whole numbers. Remember to regroup if the digit at the top is smaller than the one below it.

```
    ⁴5  ⁹0 . ⁹0  ¹0
 -   3   9 .  4   5
    ────────────────
     1   0 .  5   5
```

9 **18.3, 12.4** In the example shown on page 7, the next whole number is counted on to, then the final number is counted on to. The answers are then added together. The first calculation is: 26.7 + **0.3** = 27 and 27 + **18** = 45; **0.3** + **18** = 18.3; the second calculation is: 19.6 + **0.4** = 20 and 20 + **12** = 32; **0.4** + **12** = 12.4

10 Refer to Q8 on subtracting decimal numbers and place the larger number at the top of the calculation each time. Row 1 is 3.1 – 1.4 = **1.7**; 6.7 – 1.4 = **5.3**; Row 2 is 5.6 – 2.5 = **3.1**; 6.7 – 5.6 = **1.1**; Row 3 is 7.3 – 2.5 = **4.8**; 7.3 – 3.1 = **4.2**; 7.3 – 6.7 = **0.6**

–	2.5	3.1	6.7
1.4	1.1	1.7	5.3
5.6	3.1	2.5	1.1
7.3	4.8	4.2	0.6

11 **13.6** Refer to Focus test 1 Q9 on comparing decimal numbers; 27.3 is the largest and 13.7 is the smallest. Then refer to Q8 on subtracting decimal numbers; 27.3 – 13.7 = 13.6

12 **21.8 and 19.6** Refer to Q8 on subtracting decimal numbers. Subtract 2.2 from each number until an answer is found that is the same as one of the numbers shown in the group; 21.8 – 2.2 = 19.6

Focus test 3 (pages 8–9)

1 Multiply each number in the top row by 4 to find the number missing beneath it; divide each number in the bottom row by 4 to find the number missing above it; 8 × 4 = **32**; 28 ÷ 4 = **7**; 10 × 4 = **40**; 24 ÷ 4 = **6**; 4 × 4 = **16**

IN	3	8	7	10	6	4
OUT	12	32	28	40	24	16

2 **48** 6 × 8 = 48   3 **63** 7 × 9 = 63

4 **=, <, >** < means less than and > means greater than; 18 ÷ 2 = 9; 7 × 6 = 42 and 42 **<** 50; 56 ÷ 7 = 8 and 8 **>** 6

5 **126** 7 × 10 = 70 and 7 × 8 = 56; 70 + 56 = 126

```
  ×  | 10 | 8
  7  | 70 | 56  → 126
```

6 **144** Use column multiplication, making sure to work from right to left and add on any numbers carried over.

```
       4  8
   ×      3
   ─────────
       1  4  4
          1  2
```

7 **27 or 72** Write the answers to the 9 times table (9, 18, 27, 36, 45, 54, 63, 72, 81, 90, 99, 108) and look for digits shown on the cards; only 27 and 72 have both digits shown on the cards.

8 **260** Refer to Q6 on column multiplication; 4 × 65 = 260

9 **8** 48 is an answer in the 6 times table so invert the calculation from 48 ÷ 6 to 6 × □ = 48; 6 × **8** = 48

10 **13 r 2** 5 divides into 6 once and there is a remainder of 1, so write 1 above the 6 and carry the 7 down to form the number 17; 5 divides into 17 three times and there is a remainder of 2, so write 3 above the 7 and 2 as the remainder.

```
         1  3  r 2
      ┌─────────
    5 │ 6  7
    -   5           (5 × 1)
      ───
        1  7
        1  5        (5 × 3)
      ─────
           2
```

11–12 Refer to Q10 on long division.
11 **19 r 1** 3 divides into 5 once and there is a remainder of 2; 8 is carried down to form the number 28; 3 divides into 28 nine times and there is a remainder of 1.

```
      1  9  r 1
   3 | 5  8
   -  3         (3 × 1)
      ‾‾
      2  8
      2  7     (3 × 9)
      ‾‾‾
         1
```

12 **23 r 3** 4 divides into 9 twice and there is a remainder of 1; 5 is carried down to form the number 15; 4 divides into 15 three times and there is a remainder of 3.

```
      2  3  r 3
   4 | 9  5
   -  8         (4 × 2)
      ‾‾
      1  5
      1  2     (4 × 3)
      ‾‾‾
         3
```

Focus test 4 (pages 10–11)

1 **(2, 12), (3, 8), (4, 6)** 2 × 12 = 24; 3 × 8 = 24; 4 × 6 = 24
2 **1, 2, 3, 4, 6, 12** 1 × 12 = 12; 2 × 6 = 12; 3 × 4 = 12
3 **1, 7, 49** 1 × 49 = 49; 7 × 7 = 49
4 **2, 3, 5, 7** These are the first four numbers with only 2 factors (1 and the number itself).
5 **True** As all even numbers can be divided by 2, they will also have 2 as a factor. Therefore they cannot be prime numbers as they will have too many factors.
6 **12, 6, 18, 24** 2 × 6 = **12** and 3 × 4 = **12**; 2 × 3 = **6**; 2 × 9 = **18** and 3 × 6 = **18**; 2 × 12 = **24** and 3 × 8 = **24**
7 As 30 is a multiple of 5 and 3 it is placed in the section where the circles overlap; 25 is only a multiple of 5 so it is placed in the remainder of the left circle and 18 is only a multiple of 3 so it is placed in the remainder of the right circle. As 16 is not a multiple of 5 or 3 it is placed outside both circles.

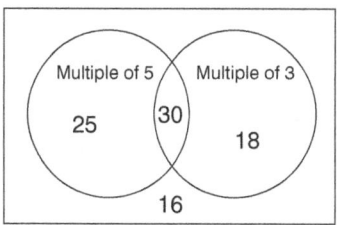

8 **56** As 7 is the larger number there will be fewer multiples of 7 between 50 and 60 than multiples of 4, so calculate this first; use times table knowledge to help (7 × 8 = 56). Check if 56 is a multiple of 4 by dividing by 4 (56 ÷ 4 = 14).
9 **8 10 ⑮ ⑨ 5 ③ ㉚** Multiples of 3 are 3 × 5 = **15**; 3 × 3 = **9**; 3 × 1 = **3**; 3 × 10 = **30**; only 3 and 5 are factors of 15 (**5** × **3** = 15).
10 Only 8 and 6 are factors of 24 (3 × **8** = 24 and 4 × **6** = 24) and only 8 and 16 are multiples of 4 (2 × 4 = **8** and 4 × 4 = **16**). The top left section shows factors of 24 that are also multiples of 4; the top right section shows factors of 24 that are not multiples of 4; the bottom left section shows numbers that are not factors of 24 but are multiples of 4; the bottom right section shows numbers that are not factors of 24 or multiples of 4.

	Multiple of 4	Not a multiple of 4
Factor of 24	8	6
Not a factor of 24	16	10

11 **1, 4, 9** 1 × 1 = 1; 2 × 2 = 4; 3 × 3 = 9
12 **16, 25, 36** 4 × 4 = 4² = **16**; 5 × 5 = 5² = **25**; 6 × 6 = 6² = **36**

Focus test 5 (pages 12–13)

1–3 To find the fraction shown on a shape, count the shaded sections to find the numerator (top number) and count all the sections to find the denominator (bottom number). If possible, simplify the fraction by dividing the numerator and denominator by the same number.

1 $\frac{1}{3}$ 2 out of 6 sections have been shaded so $\frac{2}{6}$ is shown; 2 and 6 can both be divided by 2 (2 ÷ 2 = 1 and 6 ÷ 2 = 3) so $\frac{2}{6} = \frac{1}{3}$.
2 $\frac{3}{5}$ 6 out of 10 sections have been shaded so $\frac{6}{10}$ is shown; 6 and 10 can both be divided by 2 (6 ÷ 2 = 3 and 10 ÷ 2 = 5) so $\frac{6}{10} = \frac{3}{5}$.
3 $\frac{3}{4}$ 6 out of 8 sections have been shaded so $\frac{6}{8}$ is shown; 6 and 8 can both be divided by 2 (6 ÷ 2 = 3 and 8 ÷ 2 = 4) so $\frac{6}{8} = \frac{3}{4}$.
4–5 To find fractions that have the same value (equivalent fractions), multiply the numerator and denominator by the same number. E.g. $\frac{1}{4}$ is the equivalent of $\frac{3}{12}$ as 1 × 3 = 3 and 4 × 3 = 12.
4 $\frac{8}{12}, \frac{6}{9}$ 2 × **4** = 8 and 3 × **4** = 12, so $\frac{2}{3} = \frac{8}{12}$; 2 × **3** = 6 and 3 × **3** = 9 so $\frac{2}{3} = \frac{6}{9}$.
5 $\frac{6}{20}, \frac{30}{100}$ 3 × **2** = 6 and 10 × **2** = 20, so $\frac{3}{10} = \frac{6}{20}$; 3 × **10** = 30 and 10 × **10** = 100 so $\frac{3}{10} = \frac{30}{100}$.
6 The first 2 digits after a decimal point can be written as fractions with a denominator of 100 (0.45 = $\frac{45}{100}$ and 0.54 = $\frac{54}{100}$).

Find the equivalent fraction of $\frac{1}{2}$ with a denominator of 100 by multiplying both digits by 50 (1 × 50 = 50 and 2 × 50 = 100 so $\frac{1}{2} = \frac{50}{100}$). Then compare the fractions, e.g. $\frac{45}{100}$ is less than $\frac{50}{100}$ so 0.45 is less than $\frac{1}{2}$.

	Greater than $\frac{1}{2}$	Less than $\frac{1}{2}$
0.45		✓
0.54	✓	

7 $\frac{1}{2}$ and 0.5, $\frac{3}{4}$ and 0.75, $\frac{2}{5}$ and 0.4, $\frac{3}{10}$ and 0.3, $\frac{1}{4}$ and 0.25, $\frac{9}{10}$ and 0.9 Refer to Q6 on changing decimal numbers into fractions and Q1–3 on simplifying fractions; $0.25 = \frac{25}{100}$ and this can be simplified to $\frac{1}{4}$; $0.75 = \frac{75}{100}$ and this can be simplified to $\frac{3}{4}$; 0.5 is the same as 0.50 so $0.5 = \frac{50}{100}$, $0.4 = \frac{40}{100}$, $0.9 = \frac{90}{100}$ and $0.3 = \frac{30}{100}$; $\frac{50}{100}$ can be simplified to $\frac{1}{2}$; $\frac{40}{100}$ can be simplified to $\frac{2}{5}$; $\frac{90}{100}$ can be simplified to $\frac{9}{10}$; and $\frac{30}{100}$ can be simplified to $\frac{3}{10}$.

8 **0.01**, **0.7** Refer to Focus test 1 Q9 on comparing decimal numbers.

9 $\frac{2}{5}$ Refer to Q1–3 on writing fractions shown on a shape and simplifying fractions; 4 out of 10 sections have been shaded so $\frac{4}{10}$ is shown and $\frac{4}{10} = \frac{2}{5}$ (as 4 ÷ **2** = 2 and 10 ÷ **2** = 5).

10 **40%** To change a fraction into a percentage, find the equivalent fraction with a denominator of 100; $\frac{4}{10} = \frac{40}{100}$ (as 4 × **10** = 40 and 10 × **10** = 100); the numerator shown is the same as the percentage; $\frac{40}{100} = 40\%$.

11 **Check four more squares are shaded.** $80\% = \frac{80}{100}$ and $\frac{80}{100}$ can be simplified to $\frac{8}{10}$ (refer to Q1–3 on simplifying fractions), so 8 squares should be shaded in total.

12 $\frac{1}{3}, \frac{1}{5}, \frac{3}{4}$ Refer to Q1–3 on simplifying fractions; $\frac{3}{9} = \frac{1}{3}$ (as 3 ÷ **3** = 1 and 9 ÷ **3** = 3); change 20% into a fraction by writing 20 as the numerator and 100 as the denominator ($\frac{20}{100}$) then simplify to find $\frac{20}{100} = \frac{1}{5}$; change 0.75 into a fraction by writing 75 as the numerator and 100 as the denominator ($\frac{75}{100}$) then simplify to find $\frac{75}{100} = \frac{3}{4}$.

Focus test 6 (pages 14–15)

1–2 In a sequence, if the numbers increase in size, they have been added to or multiplied; if they decrease, they have been subtracted from or divided. Check for addition or subtraction first by finding the difference between numbers next to one another. If this does not work, try multiplying or dividing a number to find an answer that is the same as a number next to it in the list.

1 **18** 54 − 45 = 9; the numbers decrease so the rule is 'subtract 9'; 27 − 9 = 18. Check this with the next number: 45 − 9 = 36, so 27 − 9 = 18.

2 **345** 195 − 145 = 50; the numbers increase so the rule is 'add 50'; 295 + 50 = 345. Check this with 195 + 50 = 245.

3 In the first row the numbers increase by 1 each time, so the rule is 'add 1'. In the second row the numbers decrease by 1 each time, so the rule is 'subtract 1'. The grid alternates these sequences on each row, so the rule for the third and fifth row is 'add 1' and the rule for the fourth row is 'subtract 1'. You could also look at this as a 'serpentine loop' counting up and the rows read from left to right, then right to left.

1	2	3	4	5	**6**	**7**	8	9	10
20	19	**18**	**17**	**16**	15	14	13	**12**	11
21	22	23	**24**	**25**	26	27	**28**	28	30
40	**39**	38	**37**	36	**35**	**34**	33	**32**	31
41	42	**43**	**44**	**45**	46	**47**	48	**49**	50

4 **3.7** Refer to Q1 on sequences, Focus test 2 Q8 on subtracting decimal numbers and Focus test 2 Q5 on adding decimal numbers; 3.1 − 2.5 = 0.6 so the rule is 'add 0.6'; check this with 4.3 + 0.6 = 4.9; 3.1 + 0.6 = 3.7.

5 **−3** 3 − 3 = 0 so the rule is 'subtract 3'; negative numbers 'mirror' whole numbers, as shown on the number line where the numbers increase in size from left to right; 0 − 3 = −3

−9 −8 −7 −6 −5 −4 −3 −2 −1 0 1 2 3 4 5 6 7 8 9

6 **76, 91** 31 − 16 = 15; the numbers increase so the rule is 'add 15'; 61 + 15 = 76 and 76 + 15 = 91.

7–8 Refer to Q5 on negative numbers.

7 **subtract 3** 8 − 5 = 3; the numbers decrease so they have been subtracted.

8 **No** 3 subtracted from −7 = **−10**; 3 subtracted from −10 = **−13** and 3 subtracted from −13 = **−16** so 15 is not in the sequence.

9 **1.7, 3.2** Refer to Focus test 2 Q8 on subtracting decimal numbers and Focus test 2 Q5 on adding decimal numbers; 1.2 − 0.7 = 0.5; the numbers increase, so the rule is 'add 0.5'; 1.2 + 0.5 = **1.7** and 2.7 + 0.5 = **3.2**.

10 $\frac{3}{4}, 1\frac{1}{2}$ The difference between 1 and $1\frac{1}{4}$ is $\frac{1}{4}$ so the rule is 'add $\frac{1}{4}$'; $\frac{1}{2}$ is the equivalent of $\frac{2}{4}$ and $\frac{2}{4} + \frac{1}{4} = \frac{3}{4}$; $1\frac{1}{4} + \frac{1}{4} = 1\frac{2}{4}$ which is equivalent to $1\frac{1}{2}$.

11 **double** or **multiply by 2** The numbers increase so they have been added to or multiplied; 1 + 1 = 2 and 2 + 1 = 3 so it cannot be addition;

1 × 2 = 2 and 2 × 2 = 4 so the rule is 'multiply by 2'.
12 **750, 900, 1050** 300 − 150 = 150; the numbers increase so the rule is 'add 150'; 600 + 150 = **750**; 750 + 150 = **900** and 900 + 150 = **1050**.

Focus test 7 (pages 16–17)

1–3 Look at the examples shown on page 16 and turn the page to look at the triangles from different angles.
1 **right-angled**
2 **equilateral**
3 **isosceles**
4 **true** Although 2 sides on an isosceles triangle are always the same size and length, the third angle can be a right angle, as shown.

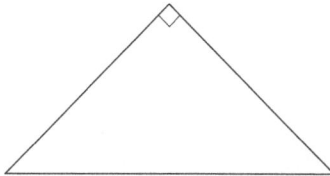

5 A quadrilateral is a 2-D shape with 4 sides.

6 **6** Lines of symmetry go through the middle of the shape, creating a 'mirror image' on each side of the line.

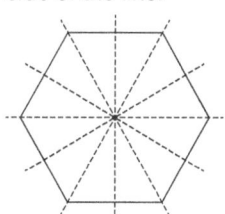

7 *Check that the quadrilateral is symmetrical.* E.g.

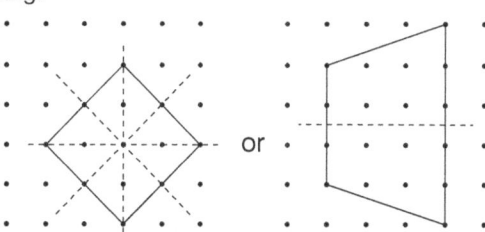

8

Name of shape	Number of faces	Number of vertices	Number of edges
Cube	6	8	12
Tetrahedron	4	4	6

9 **(triangular) prism, cylinder** Prisms are shapes with two identical faces at each end (referred to as the 'end face'). If the end of a prism were 'sliced off', the end face will always remain the same.
10 **6** A cuboid is a shape with faces that are rectangles or squares, such as a cereal packet.
11 Look at the examples shown at the bottom of page 17 to help write the answers.

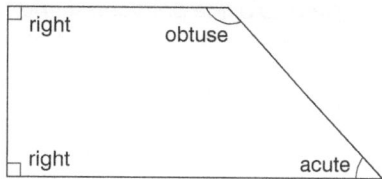

12 **Angle *a* = 135°, Angle *b* = 45°** Make sure the line along the bottom of the protractor is laid over the bottom line on the angle and the centre of the cross at the bottom of the protractor is placed over where the 2 lines meet. If the angle is larger than 90°, use the larger numbers on the protractor; if it is smaller, use the smaller numbers on the protractor.

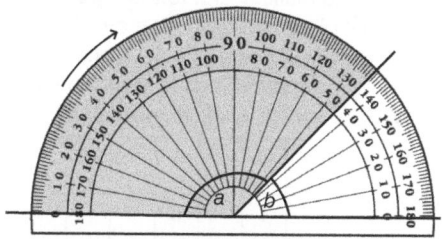

Focus test 8 (pages 18–19)

1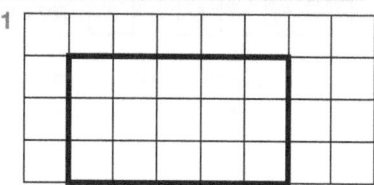

5 × 3 = 15, so the shape will be 5 squares long and 3 squares high.
2 **18 squares** Count the squares to find the area.
3 **8 cm** Write the equation as a missing number sentence ($\square$ × 6 = 48 cm²); use knowledge of the 6 times table to find the answer (**8** × 6 = 48).
4 **36 cm²** 9 × 4 = 36
5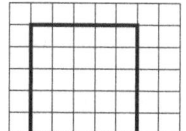

All sides on a square are equal, so the same number will be multiplied together; 5 × 5 = 25
6 **24 cm** 4 + 8 = 12; 12 × 2 = 24
7 **24 cm** 5 + 7 = 12; 12 × 2 = 24

8   **B** Shape A is 32 cm² (8 × 4 = 32); shape B is 35 cm² (5 × 7 = 35); 35 > 32
9   **120 m²** 12 × 10 = 120
10 **44 m** 12 + 10 = 22; 22 × 2 = 44
11 **3 cm** All sides on a square are equal, so the same number will be multiplied together; 3 × 3 = 9; 3 + 3 = 6 and 6 × 2 = 12
12 ***Check there is a line between A and C. Check A and B are ticked.*** The area of shape A is 24 cm² (4 × 6 = 24); the area of shape B is 25 cm² (5 × 5 = 25); the area of shape C is 24 cm² (8 × 3 = 24). The perimeter of shape A is 20 cm (4 + 6 = 10; 10 × 2 = 20); the perimeter of shape B is 20 cm (5 + 5 = 10; 10 × 2 = 20); the perimeter of shape C is 22 cm (8 + 3 = 11; 11 × 2 = 22).

Focus test 9 (pages 20–21)

1–3 To multiply or divide a number by 10, 100 or 1000, put the number in a place value grid and move it across the decimal point. Move it to the left to multiply and to the right to divide. To multiply or divide by 10 move it 1 place, by 100 move it 2 places, by 1000 move it 3 places. Below the number 1.03 is shown multiplied by 100 and 502 is shown divided by 1000.

Th	H	T	O	.	t	h	th	
			1	.	0	3		
	1	0	3	.				1.03 × 100 = 103
		5	0	2	.			
			0	.	5	0	2	502 ÷ 1000 = 0.502

1
Metres	Centimetres	Millimetres
6.5 m	**650 cm**	**6500 mm**
7.2 m	720 cm	**7200 mm**
3 m	**300 cm**	3000 mm

As 1 m = 100 cm, change metres into cm by multiplying by 100 (6.5 × 10 = 650) and to change cm into metres divide by 100 (720 ÷ 10 = 7.20). As 1 cm = 10 mm, change cm into mm by multiplying by 10 (650 × 10 = 6500) and change mm into cm divide by 10 (3000 ÷ 10 = 300).

2 **4800 ml** 1 litre = 1000 ml so multiply by 1000; 4.8 × 1000 = 4800
3 **600 g** 1 kg = 1000 g so multiply by 1000; 0.6 × 1000 = 600
4 **3400 g** Change $3\frac{1}{4}$ kg into grams to make the calculation easier; 1 kg = 1000 g, and divide by 4 to find $\frac{1}{4}$ (1000 ÷ 4 = 250); therefore $3\frac{1}{4}$ kg = 3000 g + 250 g = 3250 g and 3400 is more than 3250.

5 **85 mm, 0.8 m, 85 cm, 8.5 m** Change the lengths so they are all shown in the same unit of measurement (refer to Q1–3 on multiplying and dividing by 10 and 100). For example, change them all into centimetres by dividing measurements shown in millimetres by 10 (85 mm ÷ 10 = 8.5 cm) and multiplying those shown in metres by 100 (0.8 m × 100 = 80 cm and 8.5 m × 100 = 850 cm). Then place them in order: 85 mm (8.5 cm), 0.8 m (80 cm), 85 cm, 8.5 m (850 cm).

6 **800 ml or 0.8 litres** Each 500 ml has been separated into 5 equal parts, therefore each small line represents 100 ml (500 ml ÷ 5 = 100 ml). The grey shaded area is shown level with 800 ml; 1 litre = 1000 ml, so divide by 1000 to change into litres (800 ÷ 1000 = 0.800 and 0.800 is the same as 0.8).

7 **2500 ml or 2.5 litres or $2\frac{1}{2}$ litres** The grey shaded area is shown level with $2\frac{1}{2}$ litres; 1 litre = 1000 ml, so 500 ml = $\frac{1}{2}$ litre; 2000 ml + 500 ml = 2500 ml.

8 **37 mm, 25 mm, 4.5 cm** Count the small lines between the cm shown on the ruler to measure in mm; measure to the nearest whole cm and count the number of mm after it to find the number to insert after the decimal point.

9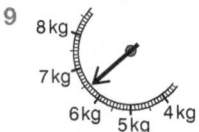

Between each kg, the scales have been separated into 10 equal parts (1 ÷ 10 = 0.1), with $\frac{1}{2}$ kg between each number shown by an extra, small line. Therefore, the arrow points to the fourth line after 6 kg.

10 **300 ml** Use knowledge of the weight of familiar items, e.g. a large bottle of water is 1.5 litres (or 1500 ml), so 300 ml is the most appropriate measurement.

11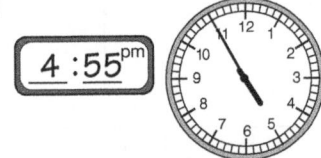

The time is 35 mins past 4 so add 20 mins to 35; 20 + 35 = 55 so it will be 4:55. Moving around a clock face, each number represents 5 minutes that have passed. Use the numbers on the clock to count up in 5s: the minute hand points to 11 to show 55 mins. The hour hand is shown just before the 5 as the hour moves from 4 to 5.

12 **8:40 p.m.** Use a number line to calculate the elapsed time, as shown; 1 hr = 60 mins so $\frac{1}{2}$ hr = 30 mins.

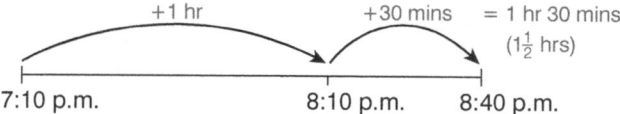

Focus test 10 (pages 22–23)

1 (–2, 2)
2 (–2, 7)
3 (3, 7)
4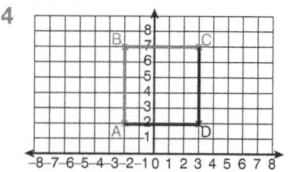
Vertices are the corners of a shape. A is 5 squares below B and C is 5 squares across from B, so count 5 squares down from C or 5 squares along from A.
5 (3, 2)
6 **Check the triangle is isosceles with two sides the same length.** For example,

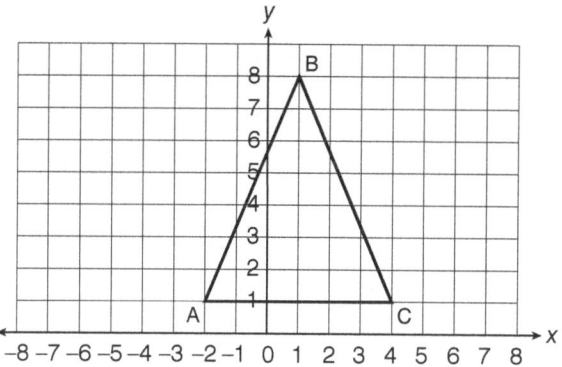

7 **Check the coordinates match the vertices of the triangle drawn.** For example, the coordinates shown on the example in Q6 are A (–2, 1), B (1, 8) and C (4, 1).
8 **reflected** A mirror image of the shape is shown, so it is a reflection.
9 **rotated** The shape has been rotated 180°.
10 **translated** The shape has been moved across the grid without being reflected or rotated so it is a translation.
11 **rotated** The tile has been rotated 90° clockwise each time.
12 **Check pattern for translation, rotation or reflection.** Refer to the explanations of rotation, reflection and translation shown on page 23.

Focus test 11 (pages 24–25)

1 Refer to the explanation of multiples on page 10. The top left section shows multiples of 3 that are odd numbers; the top right section shows multiples of 3 that are not odd numbers. The bottom left section shows numbers that are not multiples of 3 but are odd numbers; the bottom right section shows numbers that are not multiples of 3 or odd numbers.

	Odd number				Not an odd number			
Multiple of 3	3	9	15	**21**	6	12	18	**24**
Not a multiple of 3	1 5 7 11 13 17 19 **23 25**				2 4 8 10 14 16 20 **22**			

2 **4**
3 **8**
4 **17**
5–8 To read a block graph, look at the information on the left-hand side to find what each bar represents and look at the numbers along the bottom the bars are level with.
5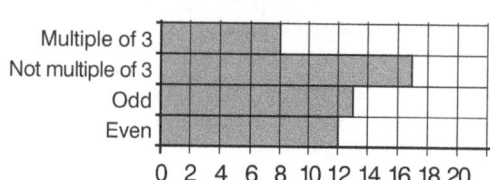

A bar should be drawn level with the 8 shown along the bottom of the graph.
6 **12** The bar representing numbers that are 'Not an odd number' is level with 12.
7 **1** The bar representing numbers that are 'Odd' is shown halfway between 12 and 14, which means there are 13; 13 –12 = 1
8 **25** 13 odd numbers + 12 even numbers = 25
9–12 To read a conversion chart, find the given measurement on the chart and use a ruler to draw a line that meets the diagonal line, as shown for question 9 overleaf (A). Draw another line (B) from that point to find the number along the other axis it is level with.

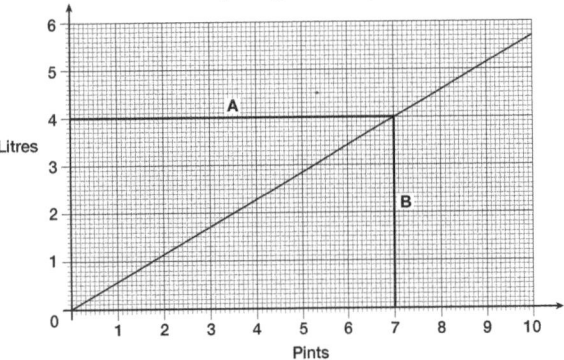

Comparing litres to pints

9 **7 pints** The part of the diagonal line 4 litres crosses is level with 7 pints.
10 **2 litres** Place the ruler vertically half way between 3 and 4 pints; the part of the diagonal line it crosses is level with 2 litres.
11 **600 ml** Convert litres into ml to make the calculation easier (1 litre = 1000 ml); between each litre, the graph is separated into 10 equal parts so divide 1000 ml by 10 (1000 ÷ 10 = 100); therefore each horizontal represents 100 ml; the part of the diagonal line 1 pint crosses with is 600 ml.
12 **5 litres** The part of the diagonal line 5 pints crosses is level with approximately 2 litres 800 ml; 5 litres is greater than 2 litres 800 ml.

Focus test 12 (pages 26–27)

1–5 Refer to the explanations of mode, median and mean on page 26.
1 **7 m** 8 + 9 + 9 + 3 + 5 + 9 + 6 = 49; 49 ÷ 7 = 7
2 **9 m** 9 m occurs most often.
3 **8 m** 3, 5, 6, 8, 9, 9, 9; the number in the middle is 8.
4 **9 m** 5, 8, 9, 9, 9; the number in the middle is 9.
5 **8 m** 8 + 9 + 9 + 5 + 9 = 40; 40 ÷ 5 = 8
6–9 Refer to the explanation on using a probability scale on page 26.
6 **good chance** There is a greater than even chance of seeing a bird, but it is not certain so it is a 'good chance'.
7
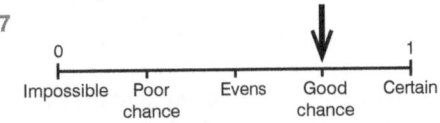
8 **poor chance** There is a less than even chance of it breaking, but it is not impossible so it is a 'poor chance'.
9
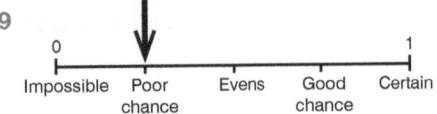

10–12 There are 8 shapes altogether, so calculate the probability out of 8 each time. If possible, simplify the answer by dividing both numbers by the same number; e.g. 6 in 8 can be simplified to 3 in 4 as both numbers can be divided by 2 (6 ÷ 2 = 3 and 8 ÷ 2 = 4).
10 **1 in 8** Only 1 triangle is shown amongst the 8 shapes.
11 **1 in 2** There are 4 circles so the probability is 4 in 8; both numbers can be divided by 4 to simplify this to 1 in 2.
12 **1 in 4** There is 1 triangle and 1 pentagon so the probability is 2 in 8; both numbers can be divided by 2 to simplify this to 1 in 4.

Mixed paper 1 (pages 28–31)

1–2 Refer to Focus test 1 Q1 on inserting missing numbers on a number line;
4000 − 3000 = 1000 and 1000 ÷ 10 = 100 so the number line increases in 100s and each small line represents 10 (100 ÷ 10 = 10).
1 **3400**
2 **3910**
3–4 Refer to Focus test 9 Q1–3 on multiplying and dividing by 10, 100 and 1000; place the numbers on the grid and count how many spaces they are moved to get the answers shown.
3 **× 10** 14.3 is moved 1 place to the left so it has been multiplied by 10.
4 **× 100** 0.5 is moved 2 places to the left so it has been multiplied by 100.
5 **7661** Complete the addition, making sure to work from right to left and to carry any numbers over.
6 **3704** Refer to Focus test 2 Q6 on column subtraction.
7 **11.2 kg** Refer to Focus test 2 Q5 on adding decimal numbers; 3.6 + 7.6 = 11.2
8 **7.5 km** Refer to Focus test 2 Q8 on subtracting decimal numbers; 12 is the same as 12.0 and 12.0 − 4.5 = 7.5.
9 **60** Write the equation as a missing number sentence: ☐ − 36 + 50 = 74. Work backwards through the equation, completing the inverse (divide instead of multiplying, subtract instead of adding, etc.): 74 − 50 = 24 and 24 + 36 = 60.

10–14

IN	5	3	**4**	9	**7**	8
OUT	30	**18**	24	**54**	42	**48**

Multiply each number in the top row by 6 to find the number missing beneath it; divide each number in the bottom row by 6 to find the number missing above it; 3 × 6 = **18**; 24 ÷ 6 = **4**; 9 × 6 = **54**; 42 ÷ 6 = **7**; 8 × 6 = **48**

15–18 Refer to the explanation of factors, prime numbers, multiples and square numbers on pages 10–11.
15 **47** The only factors of 47 are 1 and 47.
16 **49** $7 \times 7 = 7^2 = 49$
17 **45** Find the multiples of 5 first (these are easier to identify as the last digit will always be 5 or 0); 45 and 50 are the only multiples of 5; divide the numbers by 3 to find the multiple of 3; $45 \div 3 = 15$
18 **48** Work through the list, counting the factors of each number; factors of 48 are 1, 2, 3, 4, 6, 8, 12, 16, 24, 48.
19 $\frac{1}{4}$ Refer to Focus test 5 Q1–3 on finding the fraction shown on a shape and simplifying fractions; 3 grey squares have been shaded out of 12 squares so $\frac{3}{12}$ is shown; both numbers can be divided by 3, so $\frac{3}{12} = \frac{1}{4}$.
20–22 To change a percentage into a fraction, write the number as the numerator (top number) with 100 as the denominator. Refer to Focus test 5 Q1–3 on simplifying fractions.
20 $\frac{7}{10}$ $70\% = \frac{70}{100}$; both numbers can be divided by 10 so $\frac{70}{100} = \frac{7}{10}$.
21 $\frac{1}{2}$ $50\% = \frac{50}{100}$; both numbers can be divided by 50 so $\frac{50}{100} = \frac{1}{2}$.
22 $\frac{1}{5}$ $20\% = \frac{20}{100}$; both numbers can be divided by 20 so $\frac{20}{100} = \frac{1}{5}$.
23 **25** Refer to the explanation of square numbers on page 11; $4 \times 4 = 16$ so the next number to be multiplied will be 5 and $5 \times 5 = 25$.
24 **191** 190 is even as it can be divided exactly by 2, so 191 is the next odd number.
25–26 **160, 200** Refer to page 14 and Focus test 6 Q1–2 on sequences; $120 - 80 = 40$; the numbers increase so the rule is 'add 40'; $120 + 40 = 160$ and $160 + 40 = 200$.

27–29

Name of shape	Number of faces	Number of vertices	Number of edges
Cuboid	6	8	12

Refer to the explanation of properties of 3-D shapes on page 17.

30
A pentagon is a 5-sided shape and the one shown crossed out has 4 sides.
31–34 Refer to the explanations of how to find the area and perimeter on pages 18–19.
31 **63 square centimetres** $9 \times 7 = 63$
32 **32 cm** $9 + 7 = 16$; $16 \times 2 = 32$
33 **64 square centimetres** All sides are the same length on a square; $8 \times 8 = 64$

34 **32 cm** $8 + 8 = 16$; $16 \times 2 = 32$
35 **45 mm** A slightly larger line is shown at every 10 mm and the line is level with 5 mm after 40 mm; $40 + 5 = 45$
36 **150 g** Use knowledge of the weight of familiar things to help choose the correct answer. For example, a bag of sugar weighs 1 kg, which is the equivalent of 1000 g.
37 **10:40** Refer to Focus test 9 Q11 on telling the time; the minute hand points to 8 to show 40 mins. The hour hand shows about halfway between 10 and 11 (it has passed 10 but not yet reached 11).
38 **11:10** Refer to Focus test 9 Q12 on calculating elapsed time; 1 hr = 60 mins so $\frac{1}{2}$ hr = 30 mins; 10:40 to 11:00 = 20 mins; 30 mins – 20 mins = 10 mins left to add on; 11:00 + 10 mins = 11:10
39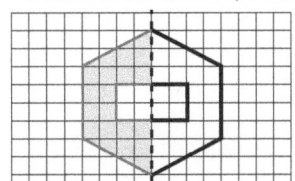
A mirror image on the other side of the dotted line should be drawn, as shown.
40–41 Refer to the explanation on how to write and plot coordinates on page 22.
40 **(3, 5)**
41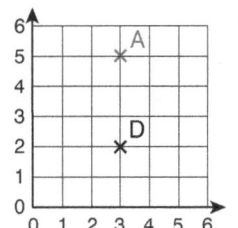
42 **South** Moving clockwise around a compass, the directions are: North, East, South, West. Point D is directly below point A so it is South.
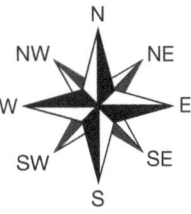
43 **16** To read a bar chart, look at the number the top of each bar is level with (it helps to place a ruler at the top of the bar to find the number). Each line between the numbers has been separated into 5 equal sections, so each line represents 1 minibeast; the bar is level with 1 line after 15 and $15 + 1 = 16$.
44 **trees** The highest bar shown is for trees, which is level with 19.

45 **6** The bar is level with 11 for flowers and with 5 for stones; 11 − 5 = 6
46 **51** 16 + 19 + 11 + 5 = 51
47–48 Refer to the explanations of mode, median and mean on page 26.
47 **6** 7 + 4 + 8 + 9 + 5 + 4 + 5 = 42; 42 ÷ 7 = 6
48 **5** 4, 5, 5, 5, 7, 8, 9; the number in the middle is 5.
49 **To have a hot day in July** The chances of a hot day in July are greater than one in December.
50 **To hear a bird sing** The chances of hearing a bird sing are greater than hearing a roll of thunder.

Mixed paper 2 (pages 32–35)

1–2 Refer to the example on page 5 of converting between decimal numbers and fractions.
1 **0.9** '0.3 is the same as $\frac{3}{10}$' therefore 0.9 is the same as $\frac{9}{10}$.
2 **0.07** '0.03 is the same as $\frac{3}{100}$' therefore 0.07 is the same as $\frac{7}{100}$.
3–4 Refer to Focus test 1 Q3 on rounding.
3 **8800 m** 8 is in the hundreds place and 4 is to its right, so 8 remains the same and the following digits change to 0.
4 **7300 m** 2 is in the hundreds place and 6 is to its right, so 2 increases by 1 and the following digits change to 0.
5 **£15.60** Refer to the example shown on page 6 on how to add decimal numbers; £7.80 + £7.80 = £15.60
6 **£4.40** Refer to Focus test 2 Q8 on subtracting decimal numbers; £20.00 − £15.60 = £4.40
7 **1334** Refer to Focus test 2 Q6 on column subtraction; 1931 − 597 = 1334
8 **3753** Refer to Focus test 1 Q2 on ordering numbers; 597 is the smallest and 4350 is the largest; 4350 − 597 = 3753
9 **6878** 4350 + 1931 + 597 = 6878
10 **148** Refer to Focus test 3 Q5 on using a grid to complete multiplication; 4 × 30 = 120 and 4 × 7 = 28; 120 + 28 = 148
11 **24 r 2** Refer to Focus test 3 Q10 on long division.
12 **300** 6 × 5 = 30 so 60 × 5 = 300.
13 **230** Use short division to find the answer; 2 divides into 4 twice so write 2 above the 4; 2 divides into 6 three times, so write 3 above it;
2 divides into 0 zero times so write 0 above it.

```
      2 3 0
    2 ) 4 6 0
```

14 **34** Use knowledge of the 4 times tables to find which numbers between 30 and 35 can be divided exactly by 4; 8 × 4 = 32 so 32 ÷ 8 = 4 and 32 + 2 = 34.
15–18 (56) **7 18 26 14** (8) Refer to the explanations of factors and multiples on page 10; **56** ÷ 4 = 14 and **8** ÷ 4 = 2; 4 × **7** = 28 and 2 × **14** = 28.
19 **75%** Refer to Focus test 5 Q1–3 on finding the fraction shown in a shape and Focus test 5 Q10 on changing fractions into percentages; 3 out of 4 sections have been shaded so $\frac{3}{4}$ is shown; multiply both numbers by 25 to find $\frac{3}{4} = \frac{75}{100}; \frac{75}{100}$ = 75%.
20–22 $\frac{1}{20} < \frac{1}{4} < \frac{9}{10}$ Refer to Focus test 5 Q4–5 on equivalent fractions. Find the largest denominator (bottom number) and find the equivalent fractions of the others that have the same denominator; $\frac{1}{20}$ has the largest denominator; $\frac{9}{10} = \frac{18}{20}$ and $\frac{1}{4} = \frac{5}{20}$; < means less than and $\frac{1}{20} < \frac{5}{20} < \frac{18}{20}$ so $\frac{1}{20} < \frac{1}{4} < \frac{9}{10}$.
23–26 Refer to Focus test 6 Q1–2 on sequences.
23 **35** 47 − 44 = 3; the numbers decrease so the rule is 'subtract 3'; 38 − 3 = 35
24 **293** 287 − 285 = 2; the numbers increase so the rule is 'add 2'; 291 + 2 = 293
25 **536** 236 − 136 = 100; the numbers increase so the rule is 'add 100'; 436 + 100 = 536
26 **1 or 1.0** 0.4 − 0.2 = 0.2; the numbers increase so the rule is 'add 0.2'; 0.8 + 0.2 = 1.0 and 1.0 is the same as 1.
27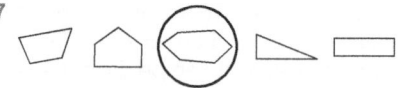
A hexagon is a 6-sided shape.
28 **4**
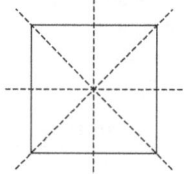
29 **prism** Refer to Focus test 7 Q9 on prisms.
30 **pyramid** A pyramid has a base and all the sides connected to the base rise to meet in a point.
31–34 Refer to the explanations of how to find the area and perimeter on pages 18–19.
31 **100 square centimetres** All sides on a square are the same length; 10 × 10 = 100
32 **40 cm** 10 + 10 = 20; 20 × 2 = 40

33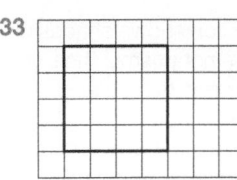

All sides on a square are the same length, so find the number that can be multiplied by itself to make 16; 4 × 4 = 16, so each side will be 4 cm.

34 **16 cm** 4 + 4 = 8; 8 × 2 = 16

35–38 **65 ml, 600 ml, 6000 ml, 6$\frac{1}{2}$ litres** Refer to page 20 and Focus test 9 Q1–3 on converting units; 1 litre = 1000 ml, so 6 litres = 6000 ml and $\frac{1}{2}$ litre = 500 ml; 6000 ml + 500 ml = 6500 ml; refer to Focus test 1 Q2 on ordering numbers.

39–42 Refer to the explanation of coordinates on page 22 and transformations on page 23.

39 **(0, 4)**

40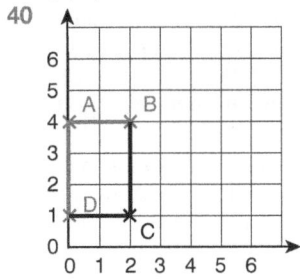

41 **(3, 1)** D is 3 squares below A and B is 2 squares across from A, so count 3 squares down from B or 2 squares across from D.

42 Refer to Focus test 10 page 23 on translated shapes.

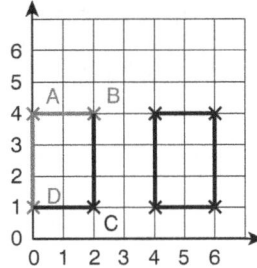

43–46 Refer to Focus test 11 Q5–8 on reading block graphs; the graph has been separated into 10 equal parts between each number so each vertical line represents 1 (10 ÷ 10 = 1).

43 **35** The grey bar for 'Children's' is level with 35.

44 **Men's** The bar for 'Men's' is level with 17.

45 **50** 15 + 35 = 50

46 **6** 23 − 17 = 6

47–48 Refer to the explanations of finding the mean and mode on page 26.

47 **8** 7 + 8 + 5 + 10 + 10 = 40; 40 ÷ 5 = 8

48 **10** 10 occurs most often.

49 **certain** A person is unable not to blink for a whole day, so it is certain.

50 **good chance** There is a greater than even chance, but it is not certain so it is a 'good chance'.

Mixed paper 3 (pages 36–39)

1–2 Refer to Focus test 1 Q9 on comparing decimal numbers; < means less than and > means greater than.

1 **>** 2 **>**

3–4 Refer to Focus test 1 Q4–5 on using a place value grid to write a number.

3 **3450**

4 **6012**

5–7

+	93	76
48	141	**124**
57	150	**133**

48 + 76 = **124**; 150 − 93 = **57**; 57 + 76 = **133**

8 **67** Write the equation as a missing number sentence: ☐ − 15 + 40 = 92. Work backwards through the equation, completing the inverse (divide instead of multiplying, subtract instead of adding, etc.): 92 − 40 = 52 and 52 + 15 = 67.

9 **10.4** Refer to Focus test 2 Q8 on subtracting decimal numbers.

10 **25 g** Refer to Mixed paper 2 Q13 on short division; 75 ÷ 3 = 25

11 **30 km** Sam makes 2 trips a day, 5 times a week; 2 × 5 = 10 and 10 × 3 km = 30 km.

12 **18** Use knowledge of times tables; all the answers in the 6 times table can be divided exactly by 6.

13 **1.5** Use short division, ensuring the decimal point is lined up in the answer; 3 divides into 4 once so write 1 above the 4; as there is a remainder of 1, carry this over to the next column to create the number 15; 3 divides into 15 five times so write 5 above it.

```
      1 . 5
   ┌────────
 3 │ 4 . ¹5
```

14 **2.5** Use column multiplication, making sure to line up the decimal point in the answer place. Work from right to left and carry any digits over, as when completing other column multiplications.

```
      0 . 5
    ×     5
    ───────
      2 . 5
      ₂
```

15–18

	Multiple of 6	Not a multiple of 6
Factor of 36	18	9
Not a factor of 36	24	13

The top left section shows factors of 36 that are also multiples of 6; the top right section shows factors of 36 that are not multiples of 6; the bottom left section shows numbers that are not factors of 36 and are multiples of 6; the bottom right section square shows numbers that are not factors of 36 or multiples of 6.

19–20 $\frac{4}{6}, \frac{6}{9}$ Refer to Focus test 5 Q4–5 on equivalent fractions; the 2 in $\frac{2}{3}$ has been multiplied by 2 to find 4 in the second fraction, so the 3 also needs to be multiplied by 2 to find the denominator (2 × 3 = 6, so it is $\frac{4}{6}$). In the third fraction the 3 in $\frac{2}{3}$ has been multiplied by 3 to find 9, so multiply 2 by 3 as well (2 × 3 = 6, so it is $\frac{6}{9}$).

21–22

	Greater than $\frac{1}{2}$	Less than $\frac{1}{2}$
0.61	✓	
0.16		✓

Refer to Focus test 5 Q6 on changing decimal numbers into fractions; 0.61 = $\frac{61}{100}$, 0.16 = $\frac{16}{100}$ and $\frac{1}{2}$ = $\frac{50}{100}$; $\frac{61}{100}$ is greater than $\frac{50}{100}$ and $\frac{16}{100}$ is less than $\frac{50}{100}$.

23–24 Refer to Focus test 6 Q1–2 on sequences.

23–24 **25, 800** The numbers increase and 50 × 2 = 100 so the rule is 'multiply by 2'; **25** × 2 = 50 and 400 × 2 = **800**.

25–26 **4, 128** The numbers increase and 8 × 2 = 16 so the rule is 'multiply by 2'; **4** × 2 = 8 and 64 × 2 = **128**.

27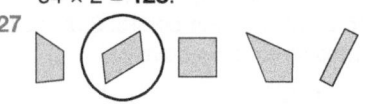

A parallelogram is a 4-sided shape with opposite sides that are parallel.

28–30

	Prism	Not a prism
Has triangular faces	C	B
Has no triangular faces	A	

Refer to Focus test 7 Q9 on prisms. The top left section shows prisms with triangular faces; the top right section shows shapes with triangular faces that are not prisms; the bottom left section shows prisms with no triangular faces; the bottom right section shows shapes that have no triangular faces and are not prisms.

31–34 Refer to the explanations on finding the area and perimeter on pages 18–19, adding decimal numbers on page 6 and multiplying decimal numbers on Mixed paper 3 Q14.

31 **15 m** 4 is the same as 4.0 and 4.0 + 3.5 = 7.5; 7.5 × 2 = 15

32 **12.4 m** 5 is the same as 5.0 and 5.0 + 1.2 = 6.2; 6.2 × 2 = 12.4

33 **A** 3.5 × 4 = 14 and 1.2 × 5 = 6; 14 > 6

34 **12 cm** All sides on a square are equal, so the same number will be multiplied together to find the area; 3 × 3 = 9 so each side is 3 cm; 3 + 3 = 6 and 6 × 2 = 12.

35 **2 m and 200 cm** Change the lengths so they are all shown in the same unit of measurement (refer to Focus test 9 Q1–3 on multiplying and dividing by 10, 100 and 1000). For example, change them all into cm by dividing measurements shown in mm by 10 (20 mm ÷ 10 = 2 cm) and multiplying those shown in metres by 100 (2 m × 100 = 200 cm and 200 m × 100 = 20 000 cm); 1 km = 1000 m, so multiply by 1000 to change into metres (2 km × 1000 = 2000 m) and then multiply the answer by 100 to change it into cm (2000 m × 100 = 200 000 cm).

36 **3500 ml** 1 litre = 1000 ml, so 3 litres = 3000 ml and 500 ml = $\frac{1}{2}$ litre; 3000 ml + 500 ml = 3500 ml.

37 **750 g** The arrow is shown halfway between 500 g and 1 kg and 1 kg = 1000 g; add the numbers together (1000 + 500 = 1500) then divide by 2 to find the number halfway between (refer to Mixed paper 2 Q13 on short division); 1500 ÷ 2 = 750

38 **1 kg 500 g** The arrow is shown pointing to 500 g after 1 kg and 1 kg + 500 = 1 kg 500 g.

39–41 Refer to the explanations of rotation, reflection and translation on page 23.

39 **rotation**
40 **translation**
41 **reflection**
42 **(3, 0)** Refer to the explanation of coordinates on page 22.

43–46 Refer to Focus test 11 Q9–12 on using conversion graphs.

43 **30 cm** The part of the diagonal line that 12 inches crosses is level with 30 cm.

44 **6 inches** The part of the diagonal line that 15 cm crosses is level with 6 inches.

45 **10 inches** 10 cm = 4 inches, so 10 inches is longer.

46 **2.5 cm or $2\frac{1}{2}$ cm** Between each cm, the graph is separated into 5 equal parts so each horizontal line represents 1 cm (5 ÷ 5 = 1); the part of the diagonal line that 1 inch crosses is level with 2.5 cm.

47–48 Refer to the explanations of mean and median on page 26.

47 **40** 40 + 30 + 60 + 40 + 30 = 200; 200 ÷ 5 = 40

48 **40** 30, 30, 40, 40, 60; the number in the middle is 40.

49 **even chance** There are an equal amount of odd and even numbers on a dice, so the chance is 'even'.

50 **poor chance** A dice has 6 sides and 1 is only on one of the sides, so the chance of throwing it is 'poor'.

Mixed paper 4 (pages 40–43)

1–4 **3.18 < 3.81 < 8.31 < 13.8** 13 is the greatest number before the decimal point, so this will be last. Refer to Focus test 1 Q9 on comparing decimal numbers and sort the rest of the numbers by looking for the smallest digit in each column.

5–8 **56 and 71, 53 and 38, 37 and 52, 49 and 64** There are 8 numbers so there will be 4 pairs; find the 4 largest numbers and subtract 15 to find the number in the group it matches.

9 **28 kg** 8.5 + 8.5 = 17 so subtract this from 45 to find the answer; 45 − 17 = 28

10 **260** Refer to Focus test 3 Q6 on column multiplication; 52 × 5 = 260

11 **26** Refer to Mixed paper 2 Q13 on short division; 78 ÷ 3 = 26

12–13 **36 and 45** Use knowledge of the 9 times table to help; 4 × 9 = 36 and 5 × 9 = 45 so these numbers can be divided exactly by 9.

14 **36** Use knowledge of the 3 and 4 times table to help; 9 × 4 = 36 and 3 × 12 = 36 so 36 can be divided exactly by 3 and 4.

15–16 Refer to the explanation of square numbers on page 11; < means less than and > means greater than.

15 **>** $5^2 = 25$ and 3 × 8 = 24; 25 > 24

16 **<** 9 × 3 = 27 and $8^2 = 64$; 27 < 64

17–18 **15, 5** Refer the explanations of factors on page 10; 2 × **15** = 30 and **5** × 6 = 30

19–20 **0.05, 0.8** Refer to Focus test 1 Q9 on comparing decimal numbers.

21–22 Refer to Focus test 5 Q10 on changing fractions into percentages.

21 **75%** $\frac{3}{4} = \frac{75}{100}$ (as 3 × **25** = 75 and 4 × **25** = 100); $\frac{75}{100} = 75\%$

22 **5%** $\frac{1}{20} = \frac{5}{100}$ (as 1 × **5** = 5 and 20 × **5** = 100); $\frac{5}{100} = 5\%$

23–26 Refer to the explanation of square numbers on page 11 and Focus test 6 Q1–2 on sequences.

23–24 **16, 49** 4 × 4 = 16 and 7 × 7 = 49

25 **1.5** 0.6 − 0.3 = 0.3; the numbers increase so the rule is 'add 0.3'; 1.2 + 0.3 = 1.5

26 **$2\frac{1}{4}$** As the equivalent of $\frac{1}{2}$ is $\frac{2}{4}$, the equivalent of $1\frac{1}{2}$ is $1\frac{2}{4}$ so the rule is 'add $\frac{1}{4}$'; $2 + \frac{1}{4} = 2\frac{1}{4}$.

27–29 Refer to the examples of angles shown on page 17.

Type of angle	Acute	Obtuse	Right
Number of angles	1	2	1

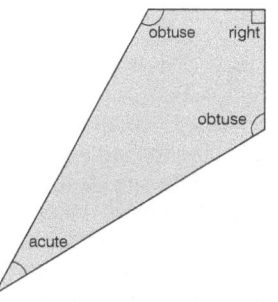

30 **6 faces** A face is a flat side of a solid object and a cube is the same shape as a dice.

31–34 Refer to the explanations on finding the area and perimeter on pages 18–19.

31 **30 cm** 8 + 7 = 15; 15 × 2 = 30

32 **30 cm** 6 + 9 = 15; 15 × 2 = 30

33 **A** Shape A is 56 cm² (8 × 7 = 56); shape B is 54 cm² (6 × 9 = 54); 56 > 54

34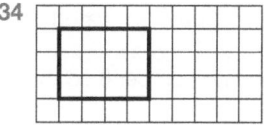

Half of 14 = 7 so 2 sides of the rectangle will add up to 7 cm. Therefore the sides could be 1 cm and 6 cm, 2 cm and 5 cm or 3 cm and 4 cm. Multiply the pairs of numbers to find which pair gives an answer of 12; 3 × 4 = 12.

35 **2 m** Use knowledge of the length of familiar items, e.g. a ruler is 30 cm; 2 m = 200 cm, so 2 m is the most appropriate measurement.

36 **2400 g** 1 kg = 1000 g, so 2 kg = 2000 g; $\frac{1}{4}$ kg = 250 g as 1000 ÷ 4 = 250; 2000 g + 250 g = 2250 g; 2250 < 2400

37–38 Between each 500 ml, the jug has been separated into 5 equal parts, so each small line represents 100 ml (500 ml ÷ 5 = 100 ml).

37 **300 ml** The grey shaded area is shown level with 300 ml.

38 **700 ml** The grey shaded area is shown level with 700 ml.

39–42 Refer to the explanation of coordinates on page 22.
39–40 (–1, 2)   (1, 2)
41–42
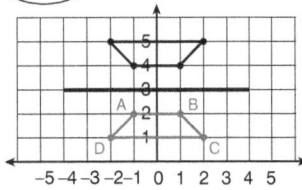
Refer to the explanation of reflections on page 23.

43–46

	Has right angles	No right angles
Quadrilateral	A G	C H
Not a Quadrilateral	B E	D F

A quadrilateral is a 4-sided shape and a right angle is 90°. The top left section shows quadrilaterals with right angles; the top right section shows quadrilaterals without right angles; the bottom left section shows shapes that are not quadrilaterals but have right angles; the bottom right section shows shapes that are not quadrilaterals and do not have right angles.

47–48 Refer to the explanations of finding the mode and mean on page 26.
  47 **30 kg** 30 kg appears the most often.
  48 **40 kg** 30 + 20 + 90 + 60 + 30 + 10 = 240; 240 ÷ 6 = 40
  49 **good chance** There are more odd numbers than even numbers so there is a 'good chance'.
  50 **impossible** There is no number 6 so this is 'impossible'.

Mixed paper 5 (pages 43–47)

1–2 Refer to Focus test 1 Q3 on rounding; as the number is being rounded to tenths, the last digit will be in the tenths place.
  1 **26.4 m** 3 is in the tenths place and 8 is to its right, so 3 increases by 1.
  2 **1.5 kg** 5 is in the tenths place and 4 is to its right, so 5 remains the same.
3–4 Refer to Focus test 1 Q12 on dividing and multiplying by 10.
  3 **3.7**   4 **50.2**
5–8 Refer to Focus test 1 Q9 on comparing decimal numbers and Focus test 2 Q5 and Q8 on adding and subtracting decimal numbers; 26.3 is the largest number and 18.8 is the smallest.

5 **7.5** 26.3 – 18.8 = 7.5
6 **45.1** 26.3 + 18.8 = 45.1
7 **52** Add the 2 largest numbers; 26.3 + 25.7 = 52
8 **0.4** Subtract each number from the largest (26.3), then subtract from the next largest (25.7) and so on; 19.2 – 18.8 = 0.4
9 **5114** 4935 + 179 = 5114
10 **245** Refer to Focus test 3 Q6 on column multiplication; 49 × 5 = 245
11 **210** Use times table knowledge; 7 × 3 = 21 so 7 × 30 = 210
12 **23** Refer to Mixed paper 2 Q13 on short division; 92 ÷ 4 = 23
13 **6** Use knowledge of the 6 times table; 6 × 6 = 36 so 36 ÷ 6 = 6
14 **2** Refer to Mixed paper 2 Q13 on short division; 50 ÷ 3 = 16 times and there is a remainder of 2.
15–18 Refer to the explanation of prime numbers, square numbers, multiples and factors on pages 10–11.
  15 **11** Only 11 has 2 factors (1 and the number itself).
  16 **81** 9 × 9 = 81
  17 **21** 7 × 3 = 21
  18 **51** As factors are pairs, multiply 3 and 17; 3 × 17 = 51
19–22 Refer to Focus test 5 Q1–3 on simplifying fractions.
  19 $\frac{2}{3}$ 10 and 15 can both be divided by 5 (10 ÷ **5** = 2 and 15 ÷ **5** = 3) so $\frac{10}{15} = \frac{2}{3}$.
  20 $\frac{4}{5}$ To change a percentage into a fraction, write the number as the numerator (top number) with 100 as the denominator; 80% = $\frac{80}{100}$ and $\frac{80}{100}$ can be simplified to $\frac{4}{5}$ (as 80 ÷ **20** = 4 and 100 ÷ **20** = 5).
  21 $\frac{3}{5}$ The first digit after a decimal point can be written as fractions with a denominator of 10; 0.6 is $\frac{6}{10}$ as a fraction; $\frac{6}{10}$ can be simplified to $\frac{3}{5}$ (as 6 ÷ **2** = 3 and 10 ÷ **2** = 5).
  22 $\frac{3}{10}$ In fractions that are equivalent of $\frac{1}{2}$ the numerator (top number) is always exactly half of the denominator (bottom number), e.g. $\frac{4}{8}$ and $\frac{5}{10}$ are both equal to $\frac{1}{2}$; therefore look for the fraction with a numerator that is less than half of its denominator.
23–26 Refer to page 14 and Focus test 6 Q1–2 on sequences.
  23 **1400** 1350 – 1300 = 50; the numbers increase so the rule is 'add 50'; 1350 + 50 = 1400
  24 **–5** Refer to Focus test 6 Q5 on negative numbers; 5 – 5 = 0 so the rule is 'subtract 5'; 0 – 5 = –5
  25 **1300** 1290 – 1280 = 10; the numbers increase so the rule is 'add 10'; 1290 + 10 = 1300

26 **14.5** 13 is the same as 13.0 and 13.0 − 11.5 = 1.5; the numbers increase so the rule is 'add 1.5'; 13.0 + 1.5 = 14.5
27 **acute** Refer to the examples of angles shown on page 17.
28 **Angle z = 130°** Refer to Focus test 7 Q12 on using a protractor.
29 **cube** A net, when cut out and folded along the lines shown, will form a 3-D shape.
30 **8 vertices** Vertices are the corners of a shape.
31–34 Refer to the explanations on finding the area and perimeter on pages 18–19.
31 *Check there is a line between A and C.* 9 × 4 = 36 and 6 × 6 = 36
32 *Check A and D are ticked.* 9 + 4 = 13 and 13 × 2 = 26; 6 + 7 = 13 and 13 × 2 = 26
33 **8 cm** Write the equation as a missing number sentence (☐ × 4 = 32) and use knowledge of the 4 times table; **8** × 4 = 32
34 **290 m²** Calculate the area of each rectangle then add the answers together; 5 × 30 = 150; 7 × 20 = 140; 150 + 140 = 290
35 **18 cm** The end of the third pencil is shown level with 18 cm on the ruler.
36 **24 cm** The end of the first pencil is shown level with 6 cm on the ruler, so add another 6 cm to 18 cm (6 + 18 = 24) or multiply 6 by 4 (6 × 4 = 24).
37 **8000 g** 1 kg = 1000 g so 8 kg = 8000 g.
38 **4500 ml** 1 litre = 1000 ml, so 4 litres = 4000 ml and ½ litre = 500 ml; 4000 ml + 500 ml = 4500 ml.
39–40 Refer to the explanations of translation, rotation and reflection on page 23.
39 **rotation**
40 **translation**
41–42 Refer to the explanation of coordinates on page 22.
41 **(−3, 4)**
42
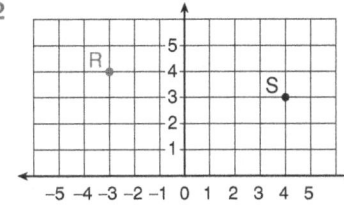
43–46 Refer to Mixed paper 1 Q43 on reading bar charts; although the bars look more like lines, the chart is read in the same way.
43 **Thursday** Only the bar for Thursday is level with 30.
44 **Monday** 30 − 5 = 25 and only the bar for Monday is level with 25.
45 **27** Between each number, the graph is separated into 5 equal parts so each horizontal line represents 1 child (5 ÷ 5 = 1); the bar is level with 2 lines after 25 and 25 + 2 = 27.

46 **2** Tuesday = 29 and Wednesday = 27; 29 − 27 = 2
47–48 Refer to the explanations of mode and mean on page 26.
47 **5p** There are more 5p coins than any other.
48 **10p** 5 + 10 + 10 + 5 + 20 + 5 + 20 + 5 + 10 = 90; 90 ÷ 9 = 10
49–50 There are 6 beads altogether, so calculate the probability out of 6 each time. If possible, simplify the answer by dividing both numbers by the same number; e.g. 6 in 8 can be simplified to 3 in 4 as both numbers can be divided by 2 (6 ÷ 2 = 3 and 8 ÷ 2 = 4).
49 **1 in 6** There is only 1 white bead out of the 6 beads.
50 **1 in 2** There are 3 black beads so the probability is 3 in 6; both numbers can be divided by 3 to simplify this to 1 in 3.

Mixed paper 6 (pages 48–52)

1–2 **8.08, 10.8** Refer to Focus test 1 Q9 on comparing decimal numbers.
3 **63 551** 4 is in the hundreds place so increase this digit by 1.
4 **72 109** The first 0 is in the hundreds place so increase this digit by 1.
5 **2214** 1364 + 850 = 2214
6 **1259** Refer to Focus test 2 Q6 on column subtraction; 2029 − 770 = 1259
7–9 Refer to Focus test 2 Q1–2 on completing column additions with missing digits.

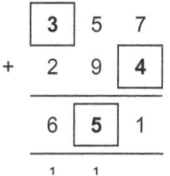

10–12 Refer to Mixed paper 2 Q13 on short division; < means less than and > means greater than.
10 **=** 52 ÷ 4 = 13
11 **<** 9 × 5 = 45; 45 < 49
12 **>** 81 ÷ 3 = 27; 27 > 26
13 **£88** Find the cost of one chair, then multiply the answer by 4; 66 ÷ 3 = 22 and 22 × 4 = 88.
14 **12** Find how many balloons there are in total and divide the answer by 3; 9 × 4 = 36 and 36 ÷ 3 = 12.
15–18 Refer to the explanation of multiples, square numbers and prime numbers on pages 10–11.
15 **35** 7 × 5 = 35
16 **6** Multiply 2 and 3 together to find the answer; 2 × 3 = 6
17 **52** 4 × 4 = 16 and 6 × 6 = 36; 16 + 36 = 52
18 **23 or 29** Between 20 and 30, only 23 and 29 have 2 factors (1 and the number itself).

19–21 Refer to Focus test 5 Q1–3 on finding the fraction shown on a shape and simplifying fractions; A = $\frac{7}{10}$, B = $\frac{5}{10}$, C = $\frac{6}{10}$ and D = $\frac{3}{10}$.

19 **B** The first digit after a decimal point can be written as fractions with a denominator of 10; 0.5 is $\frac{5}{10}$ as a fraction which is the amount of the shape that is shaded.

20 **A** To change a percentage into a fraction, write the number as the numerator (top number) with 100 as the denominator; 70% = $\frac{70}{100}$ and $\frac{70}{100}$ can be simplified to $\frac{7}{10}$ (as 70 ÷ **10** = 7 and 100 ÷ **10** = 10).

21 **C** Multiply both numbers by 2 to change $\frac{3}{5}$ into a fraction with a denominator of 10; **2** × 3 = 6 and **2** × 5 = 10 so $\frac{3}{5}$ = $\frac{6}{10}$.

22 **6** '$\frac{1}{4}$ of' means the same as '$\frac{1}{4}$ ×' and this is the same as diving by 4; 24 ÷ 4 = 6

23–24 **86, 80** Refer to Focus test 6 Q1–2 on sequences; 77 – 74 = 3; the numbers decrease so the rule is 'subtract 3'; 89 – 3 = 86 and 83 – 3 = 80.

25–26 **100, 36** Refer to the explanation of square numbers on page 11; 10 × 10 = 100 and 6 × 6 = 36.

27 **isosceles** Refer to the explanation of different types of triangles on page 16.

28 **Angle b = 70°** Two of the angles will be the same as it is an isosceles and angles in a triangle add up to 180°; 40 + 70 + **70** = 180

29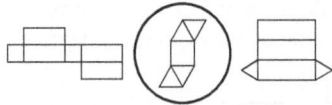

A pyramid has a base and all the sides connected to the base rise to meet in a point; the sides are the same shape as each other but can be different from the base.

30 **4 faces** A tetrahedron is a triangular based pyramid, so all 4 sides will be triangular.

31–34 Refer to the explanations on finding the area and perimeter on pages 18–19.

31 **34 cm** 12 + 5 = 17 and 17 × 2 = 34

32 **A and B have the same length perimeter.** 6 + 3 = 9 and 2 × 9 = 18; 4 + 5 = 9 and 2 × 9 = 18

33 **2 m²** A is 18 m² (6 × 3 = 18) and B is 20 m² (4 × 5 = 20); 20 – 18 = 2

34 **48 m²** 8 × 6 = 48

31–34 Between each 500 ml, the jug has been separated into 5 equal parts, therefore each small line represents 100 ml (500 ml ÷ 5 = 100 ml). On the first jug the grey shaded area is shown level with 400 ml and on the second jug it is level with 500 ml (1 litre = 1000 ml and 1000 ÷ 2 = 500).

35 **100 ml** 500 – 400 = 100
36 **900 ml** 500 + 400 = 900
37 **3500 g** 1 kg = 1000 g so 2 kg = 2000 g; 2000 + 1500 = 3500
38 **10:55 a.m.** Count back to 11:00 by subtracting 10 mins; 15 – 10 = 5 mins left to subtract; 5 mins before 11 is 10:55. One way to solve this could be to count backwards using a number line like the one in Focus test 9 Q12.

39–41 Refer to the explanation of coordinates on page 22.

39 **(5, 0)**   40 **(0, 2)**

41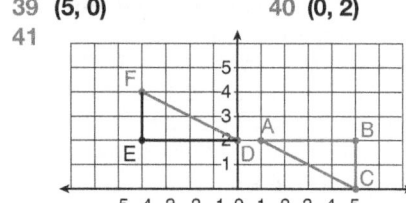

42 **rotation** Refer to the explanations of reflection, rotation and translation on page 23.

43–46 Between each kg, the graph is separated into 10 equal parts so each horizontal line represents 1 kg (10 ÷ 10 = 1).

43 **2 kg** The part of the line that 1 month crosses is level with 2 kg.

44 **3 months** The part of the line that 15 kg crosses is level with 3 months.

45 **1 kg** Month 9 = 45 kg and month 10 = 46 kg; 46 – 45 = 1. The graph shows that the line at 10 months is only 1 division (1 kg) higher than at 9 months.

46 **2–3 months** The steepest part of the graph (therefore greatest increase) is shown between 2 and 3 months.

47–48 Refer to the explanations of median and mean on page 26.

47 **11 cm** 8 cm, 9 cm, 11 cm, 12 cm, 20 cm; the number in the middle is 11 cm.

48 **12 cm** 12 + 9 + 11 + 8 + 20 = 60; 60 ÷ 5 = 12

49–50 There are 4 coins altogether, so calculate the probability out of 4 each time. If possible, simplify the answer by dividing both numbers by the same number; e.g. 6 in 8 can be simplified to 3 in 4 as both numbers can be divided by 2 (6 ÷ 2 = 3 and 8 ÷ 2 = 4).

49 **1 in 2** There are two 5p coins so the probability is 2 in 4; both numbers can be divided by 2 to simplify this to 1 in 2.

50 **1 in 4** There is only 1 20p amongst the 4 coins so it is 1 in 4.

7 Draw an arrow on this probability scale to show your answer to question 6.

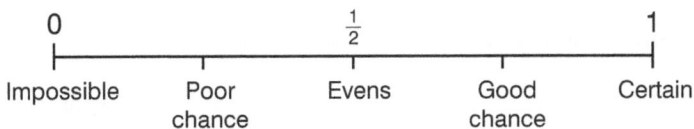

8 What is the chance that the chair you are sitting on will break today? Underline the answer.

impossible   poor chance   even chance   good chance   certain

9 Draw an arrow on this probability scale to show your answer to question 8.

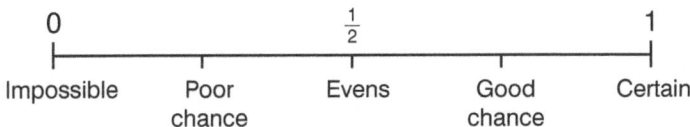

All these 2-D shapes are placed in a bag and one is picked out at random each time, then replaced in the bag.

Write **1 in 2**, **1 in 3**, **1 in 4** or **1 in 8** for each question.

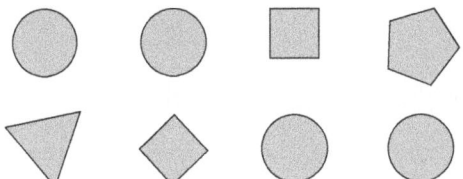

There is a 1 in 4 chance of picking a square: 2 out of 8 shapes.

10 What is the probability of picking a triangle out of the bag? _____

11 What is the probability of picking a circle out of the bag? _____

12 What is the probability of picking either a triangle or a pentagon? _____

Now go to the Progress Chart to record your score!   Total   12

Mixed paper 1

1–2 Write the number for each arrow on this number line.

Write × **10** or × **100** to make each statement true.

3 14.3 _____ = 143

4 0.5 _____ = 50

Complete these calculations.

5 2 9 0 3
   + 4 7 5 8
   _____

6 6 5 8 3
   − 2 8 7 9
   _____

7 What is the total weight of two boxes weighing 3.6 kg and 7.6 kg? _____ kg

8 What is the difference between 4.5 km and 12 km? _____ km

9 I am thinking of a number.

If I take away 36 and add 50 the answer is 74.

What is the number I am thinking of? _____

10–14 This is a 'multiply by 6' machine. Write the missing numbers in the chart.

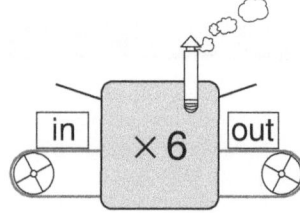

IN	5	3	__	9	__	8
OUT	30	__	24	__	42	__

Choose from these numbers to answer each question.

45   46   47   48   49   50   51

15 Which number is a prime number? _____

16 Which number is a square number? _____

17 Which number is a multiple of 3 and 5? _____

18 Which number has 10 factors, including 1 and itself? _____

19 What fraction of this shape is shaded? Circle the answer.

$\frac{1}{2}$ $\frac{3}{10}$ $\frac{1}{3}$ $\frac{1}{4}$ $\frac{3}{4}$

Write these percentages as fractions in their lowest terms.

20 70% = _____   21 50% = _____   22 20% = _____

23 What is the next square number after 16? _____

24 What is the next odd number after 189? _____

25–26 Write the missing numbers in this sequence.

80   120   _____   _____   240   280

27–29 Complete this chart.

Name of shape	Number of faces	Number of vertices	Number of edges
Cuboid	_____	_____	_____

30 Cross out the shape that is **not** a pentagon.

Calculate the area and perimeter for each of these shapes.

31 Area = _____ square centimetres

32 Perimeter = _____ cm

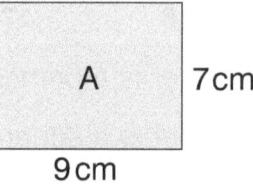

33 Area = _____ square centimetres

34 Perimeter = _____ cm

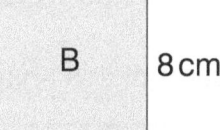

35 What is the length of this line in millimetres? _____ mm

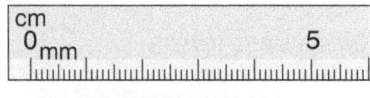

36 What is the most likely weight of an apple? Circle the answer.

        5 kg   150 g   1500 g   1 kg   5 g

37 What time is shown on this clock? _____

38 What will the time be half an hour later? _____

39 Draw the reflection of this shape. The dotted line is the mirror line.

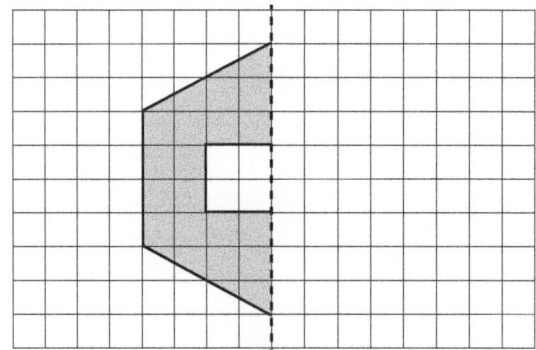

40 What are the coordinates of point A? (____, ____)

41 Point D is at (3, 2). Plot this point and label it.

42 If you stood at point A and faced point D, which direction would you face? Circle your answer.

North   South   West   East

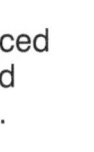 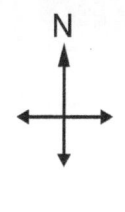

Some children counted the number of minibeasts living in different habitats.

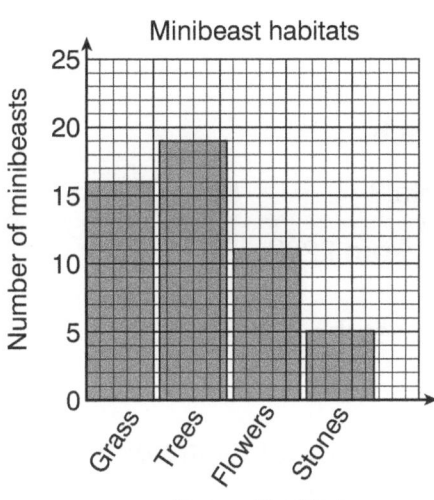

43 How many minibeasts were found in the grass? ____

44 What type of habitat were most minibeasts living in? ____

45 How many more minibeasts were found living on the flowers than the stones? ____

46 How many minibeasts were found in total? ____

Look at this set of numbers:

47 What is the mean? ____

48 What is the median? ____

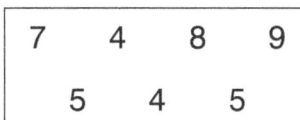

In each question, tick the statement that is more likely.

49 To have a hot day in July   OR   To have a hot day in December

50 To hear a bird sing   OR   To hear a roll of thunder

Mixed paper 2

Circle the number that is the same value as each fraction.

1 $\frac{9}{10}$ 90   9   0.9   0.09

2 $\frac{7}{100}$ 700   70   0.7   0.07

Round each length to the nearest 100 m.

3 8844 m   _____ m

4 7266 m   _____ m

Hannah buys two T-shirts for £7.80 each.

5 How much did she spend in total?   £_____

6 How much change did she get from £20?   £_____

Look at these three numbers and answer the questions.

    4350   1931   597

7 What is the difference between the two odd numbers? _____

8 What is the difference between the smallest number and the largest number? _____

9 What is the total of all three numbers? _____

10 Use this grid to multiply 37 by 4.

×	30	7
4		

11 3) 74   r _____

12 Multiply 60 by 5. _____

13 Divide 460 by 2. _____

14 Which number between 30 and 35 has a remainder of 2 when divided by 4? _____

15–18 Circle all the multiples of 4 and underline all the factors of 28.

      56   7   18   26   14   8

19 What percentage of this shape is shaded? _____%

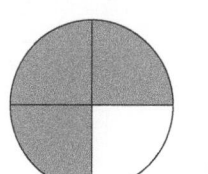

20–22 Write these fractions in order, starting with the smallest.

$\frac{9}{10}$ $\frac{1}{20}$ $\frac{1}{4}$ _____ < _____ < _____

Write the next number in each sequence.

23 47   44   41   38   _____

24 285   287   289   291   _____

25 136   236   336   436   _____

26 0.2   0.4   0.6   0.8   _____

27 Circle the shape that is a hexagon.

  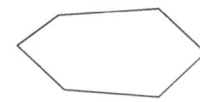 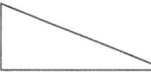 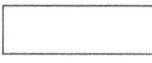

28 How many lines of symmetry does a square have? _____

Write the name for each of these shapes: **pyramid** or **prism**.

29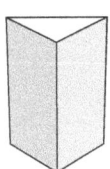
         _____

30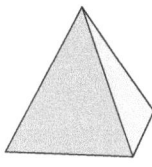
         _____

What are the area and perimeter of this square?

31 Area = _____ square centimetres

32 Perimeter = _____ cm

10 cm

33 Draw a square with an area of 16 square centimetres. Use a ruler.

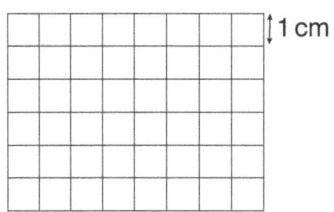

34 What is the perimeter of the square you have drawn? _____ cm

35–38 Write these amounts in order, starting with the smallest.

600 ml   6½ litres   6000 ml   65 ml

_____   _____   _____   _____

Smallest →

39 Write the coordinates of point A. (____, ____)

40 Point C is the missing corner of this rectangle at (2, 1). Plot point C and draw two lines to complete the rectangle.

41 Circle the coordinates that are **not** inside the rectangle.

(1, 2)   (3, 1)   (1, 3)

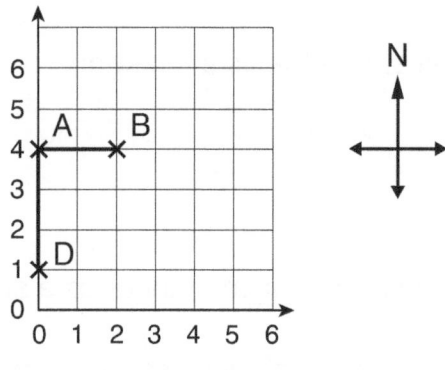

42 Translate the rectangle 4 units east and draw its new position.

This graph shows how many clothes of each type were sold in a shop over one week.

43 How many children's clothes were sold in this week? _____

44 Of which type of clothes were 17 items sold? _____

45 How many sports clothes and children's clothes were sold in total?
_____

46 How many more women's clothes than men's clothes were sold?
_____

These are David's maths test results.

Monday	Tuesday	Wednesday	Thursday	Friday
7	8	5	10	10

47 What is his mean test result? _____

48 What is his mode test result? _____

Underline the chance of each of these things happening.

49 What is the chance that you will blink today?

> impossible   poor chance   even chance
> good chance   certain

50 What is the chance you will go to bed before midnight?

> impossible   poor chance   even chance
> good chance   certain

Now go to the Progress Chart to record your score!   Total   50

Mixed paper 3

Write < or > to make each number sentence true.

1 9.14 _____ 4.9   **2** 6.08 _____ 0.86

Read these and write each as a number.

3 three thousand four hundred and fifty _____

4 six thousand and twelve _____

5–7 Write the missing numbers in this addition grid.

+	93	76
48	141	___
___	150	

8 I am thinking of a number. If I subtract 15 and add 40 my answer is 92. What number am I thinking of? _____

9 Work out 36.1 − 25.7 = _____

10 Three small cakes weigh 75 g. What is the weight of one cake? _____ g

11 Sam lives 3 kilometres from school. How many kilometres does he travel to and from school in a week, from Monday to Friday? _____ km

12 Circle the number that can be divided exactly by 6.

    26   20   44   18   52   34

Circle the correct answer for each of these.

13 4.5 ÷ 3 =   0.5   0.8   1.5   1.4   2.5

14 0.5 × 5 =   2   2.5   5   5.2   5.5

15–18 Write each number in the correct place on this Carroll diagram.

13   24   9   18

	Multiple of 6	Not a multiple of 6
Factor of 36		
Not a factor of 36		

19–20 Complete this equivalent fraction chain.

$$\frac{2}{3} = \frac{4}{\Box} = \frac{\Box}{9}$$

21–22 Use ticks to complete this chart.

	Greater than $\frac{1}{2}$	Less than $\frac{1}{2}$
0.61		
0.16		

Write the missing numbers in these sequences.

23–24 _____   50   100   200   400   _____

25–26 _____   8   16   32   64   _____

27 Circle the shape that is a parallelogram.

28–30 Write the letter of each shape in the correct place on this Carroll diagram.

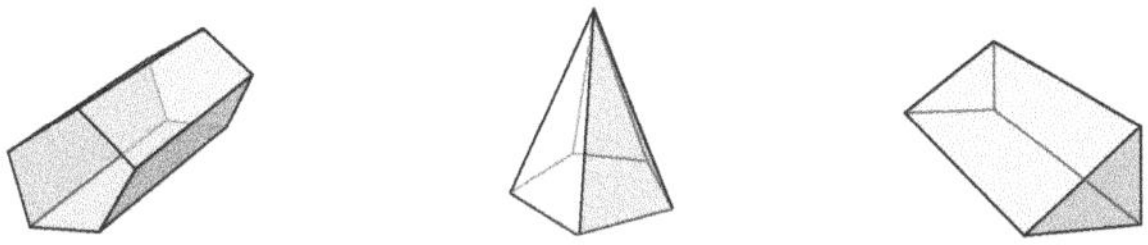

A   B   C

	Prism	Not a prism
Has triangular faces		
Has no triangular faces		

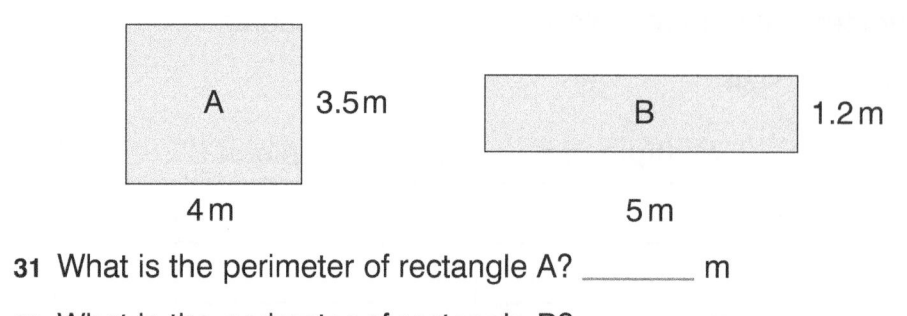

31 What is the perimeter of rectangle A? _____ m

32 What is the perimeter of rectangle B? _____ m

33 Which rectangle has the greater area, A or B? _____

34 What is the perimeter of a square with an area of 9 cm²? _____ cm

35 Circle the two measurements that are the same length.

20 mm   2 m   2 km   200 m   200 cm

36 How many millilitres are there in $3\frac{1}{2}$ litres? _____ ml

Write the weight shown on each scale.

37

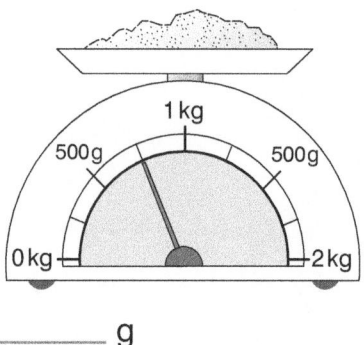

_____ g

38

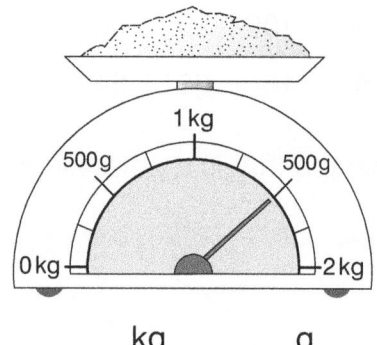

_____ kg _____ g

Write **translation**, **rotation** or **reflection** to describe the movement of the letter A in each of these diagrams.

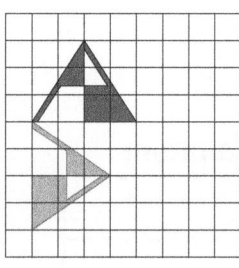

39 _____

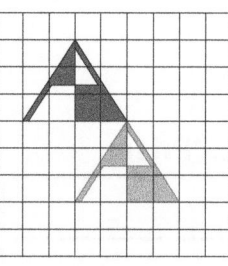

40 _____

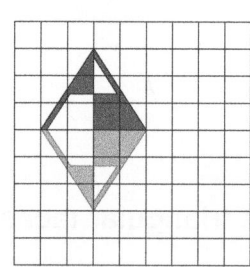

41 _____

42 Circle the coordinates that show the correct position of point Z.

(3, 1)   (0, 3)   (3, 0)   (1, 3)

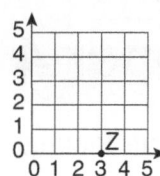

This conversion chart shows equivalent lengths in centimetres and inches.

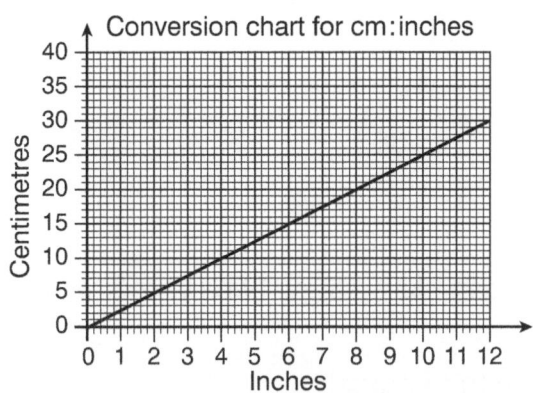

43 When inches were used in schools a ruler was 12 inches long. Approximately how long would the ruler be in centimetres? _____ cm

44 Today some rulers are 15 cm long. Approximately how long would a 15 cm ruler be in inches? _____ inches

45 Which is longer, 10 inches or 10 centimetres? _____

46 Approximately how long is 1 inch? _____ cm

Calculate the mean and median of this set of numbers.

47 Mean = _____

48 Median = _____

40	30	
60	40	30

49 What is the chance of rolling an odd number? Underline the answer.

impossible   poor chance   even chance   good chance   certain

50 What is the chance of rolling a 6? Underline the answer.

impossible   poor chance   even chance   good chance   certain

Now go to the Progress Chart to record your score!   Total

Mixed paper 4

1–4 Write this set of decimals in order, starting with the smallest.

   8.31   **13.8**   **3.18**   **3.81**

   _____ < _____ < _____ < _____

5–8 Join pairs of numbers with a difference of 15.

   56   53   38   37   64
      52   71   49

9 The total weight of three parcels is 45 kg. Two parcels weigh 8.5 kg each.

   What is the weight of the third parcel? _____ kg

10 Multiply 52 by 5. _____   **11** Divide 78 by 3. _____

Look at these numbers and answer the questions.

   15   28   36   45

12–13 Which two numbers can be divided exactly by 9? _____ and _____

14 Which number can be divided exactly by both 3 and 4? _____

Write <, > or = to make each statement true.

15 5^2 _____ 3×8 **16** 9×3 _____ 8^2

17–18 Write the missing factors for 30.

   $30 \rightarrow$ (1, 30)   (2, _____)   (3, 10)   (_____, 6)

19–20 Circle the smallest decimal and underline the largest decimal.

   0.75   0.5   0.25   0.05   0.8   0.28

Change these fractions to percentages.

21 $\frac{3}{4} =$ _____%   **22** $\frac{1}{20} =$ _____%

Write the missing square numbers in this sequence.

23–24   4   9   _____   25   36   _____   64   81

40

Write the next number in each sequence.

25   0.3   0.6   0.9   1.2   _____

26   $1\frac{1}{4}$ $1\frac{1}{2}$ $1\frac{3}{4}$ 2   _____

27–29 Look at this kite and complete the chart.

Type of angle	Acute	Obtuse	Right
Number of angles	___	___	___

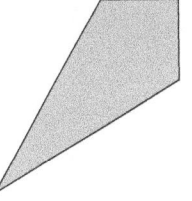

30 How many faces are there on a cube? _____ faces.

Calculate the perimeter of each rectangle.

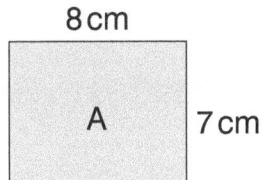
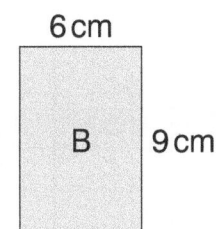

31 Perimeter of A = _____ cm   32 Perimeter of B = _____ cm

33 Which shape has the larger area, A or B? _____

34 Draw a rectangle on the grid below with a perimeter of 14 cm and an area of 12 square centimetres. Use a ruler.

35 What is the most likely height of a door? Circle the answer.

   20 cm   2 m   2 km   200 mm

36 Which is heavier, $2\frac{1}{4}$ kg or 2400 g? _____

How much water is there in each jug?

37

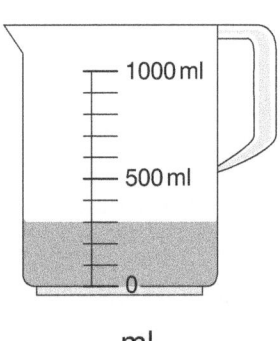

_____ ml

38

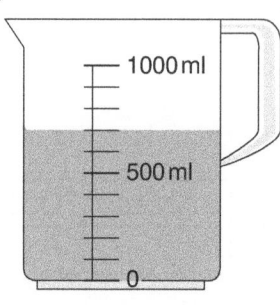

_____ ml

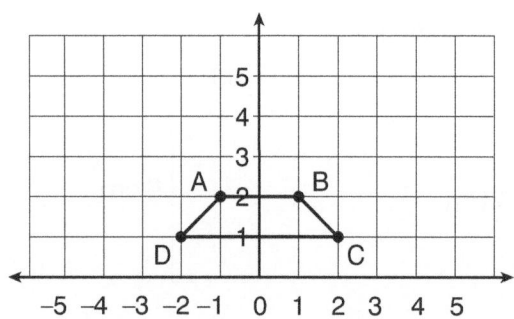

39–40 Circle the coordinates of A and underline the coordinates of B.

(2, −1)   (2, 1)   (−2, 1)   (1, 2)   (−1, 2)   (1, −2)

41–42 Draw a line from (−4, 3) to (4, 3). Use this line as a mirror line and reflect the quadrilateral ABCD.

43–46 Write the letters for shapes E, F, G and H in the correct place on this Carroll diagram.

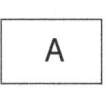 

  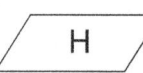

	Has right angles	**Has no right angles**
Quadrilateral	A	C
Not a quadrilateral	B	D

These are the weights of six sacks.

30 kg   20 kg   90 kg   60 kg   30 kg   10 kg

47 What is the mode weight? _____ kg

48 What is the mean weight? _____ kg

Circle the chance of spinning each number.

49 What is the chance of spinning an odd number?

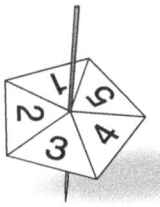

> impossible   poor chance   even chance
> good chance   certain

50 What is the chance of spinning a 6?

> impossible   poor chance   even chance
> good chance   certain

Now go to the Progress Chart to record your score!   Total   50

Mixed paper 5

Round each amount to the nearest tenth.

1 26.38 m   _____ m   **2** 1.54 kg   _____ kg

Complete these calculations.

3 37 ÷ 10 = _____   **4** 5.02 × 10 = _____

Look at these decimal numbers.

19.2   26.3   18.8   25.7

5 What is the difference between the largest and smallest number?
_____

6 What is the total of the largest and smallest number? _____

7 What is the largest total that can be made from adding any two of these numbers? _____

8 What is the smallest difference that can be made between any two numbers? _____

Complete these calculations.

9 4935 + 179 = _____

10 49 × 5 = _____

11 7 × 30 = _____

12 92 ÷ 4 = _____

13 36 ÷ 6 = _____

14 What is the remainder when 50 is divided by 3? _____

Choose from these numbers to answer each question.

    11   **21**   **81**   **51**

15 Which number is a prime number? _____

16 Which number is a square number? _____

17 Which number is a multiple of 7? _____

18 Which number has these factors: 1, 3, 17 and itself? _____

Look at these fractions.

$$\frac{3}{4} \qquad \frac{3}{5} \qquad \frac{2}{3} \qquad \frac{4}{5} \qquad \frac{3}{10}$$

19 Which fraction is equivalent to $\frac{10}{15}$? _____

20 Which fraction has the same value as 80%? _____

21 Which fraction has the same value as 0.6? _____

22 Which fraction is less than $\frac{1}{2}$? _____

Write the missing number in each sequence.

23 1300   1350   _____   1450   1500

24 5   0   _____   −10   −15

25 1280   1290   _____   1310   1320

26 11.5   13   _____   16   17.5

Look at this quadrilateral.

27 What type of angle is angle *y*?
Circle the answer.

acute   reflex   right   obtuse

28 Use a protractor to measure angle *z* accurately. Angle *z* = _____°

29 What shape will be made when this net is folded? _____

30 When the net is folded, how many vertices will the shape have?

_____ vertices

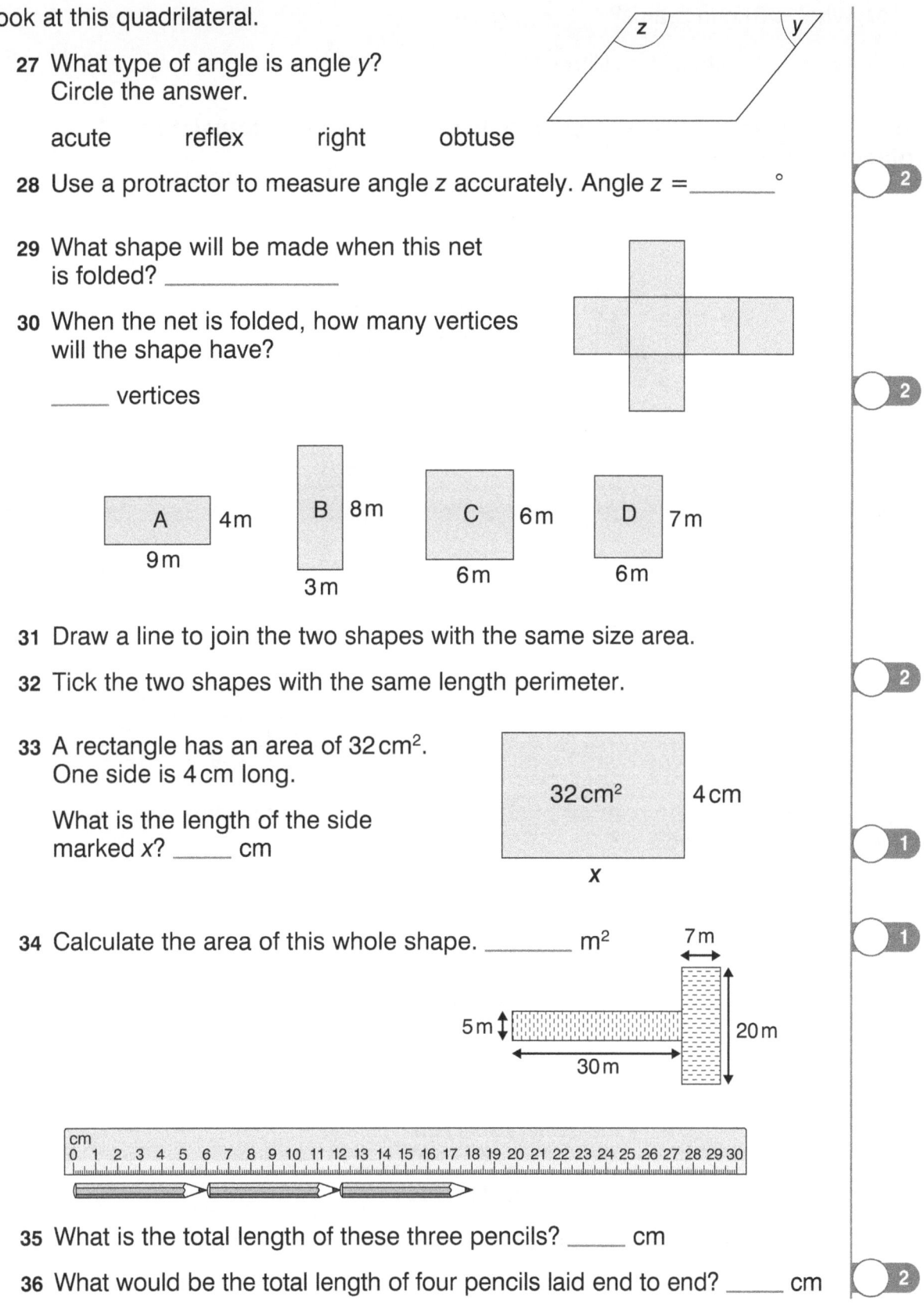

31 Draw a line to join the two shapes with the same size area.

32 Tick the two shapes with the same length perimeter.

33 A rectangle has an area of 32 cm². One side is 4 cm long.

What is the length of the side marked *x*? _____ cm

34 Calculate the area of this whole shape. _____ m²

35 What is the total length of these three pencils? _____ cm

36 What would be the total length of four pencils laid end to end? _____ cm

45

37 What is 8 kg in grams? _____ g

38 What is $4\frac{1}{2}$ litres in millilitres? _____ ml

Look at triangles A, B and C. Complete the sentences using **translation**, **rotation** or **reflection**.

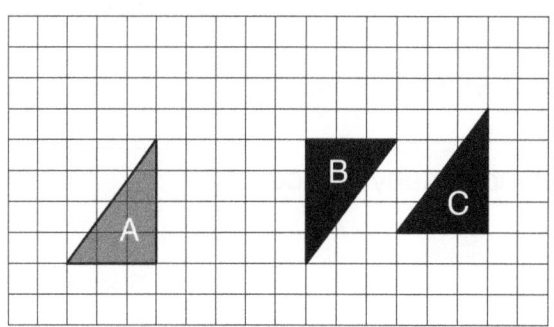

39 Triangle B is a _____ of triangle A.

40 Triangle C is a _____ of triangle A.

41 Write the coordinates of point R.

(____, ____)

42 Point S is at (4, 3). Plot this point and label it.

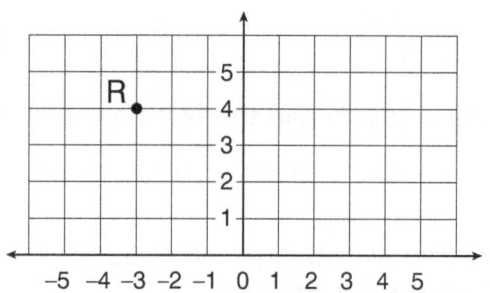

This bar chart shows the number of children from Class F that were in school on each day of the week.

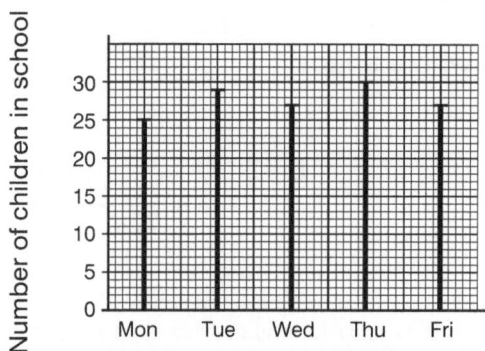

43 There are 30 children in Class F. On which day was everyone at school? _____

44 Which day were there five children away from school? _____

45 How many children were in school on Friday? _____

46 How many more children were at school on Tuesday than Wednesday? _____

What is the mode and mean of these coins?

47 Mode = _____ p   48 Mean = _____ p

In a bag there are 3 black beads, 2 grey beads and 1 white bead.

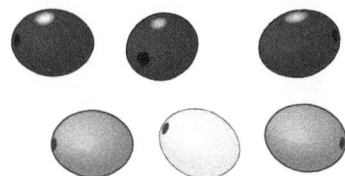

49 What is the probability of picking a white bead? Circle the answer.

   1 in 2   1 in 3   1 in 5   1 in 6

50 What is the probability of picking a black bead? Circle the answer.

   1 in 2   1 in 3   1 in 5   1 in 6

Mixed paper 6

1–2 Circle the largest number and underline the smallest number in this set.

10.08 8.1 8.08 8.11 10.8 2

Write the number that is 100 more than each of these.

3 63 451 ________

4 72 009 ________ 2

5 What is 850 more than 1364? ______

6 What is 770 less than 2029? ______ 2

7–9 The digits 3, 4 and 5 are missing. Complete this addition by writing the digits in the correct place.

$$\begin{array}{r} \square\ 5\ 7 \\ +\ 2\ 9\ \square \\ \hline 6\ \square\ 1 \\ \hline \end{array}$$

3

Write =, < or > to make each statement true.

10 $52 \div 4$ ____ 13

11 9×5 ____ 49

12 $81 \div 3$ ____ 26 3

13 Three chairs cost £66. How much will four chairs cost? £______ 1

14 There are 9 balloons in a pack and 4 packs are bought for a party. There is the same number of balloons in 3 different colours.

How many balloons are there of each colour? ____ 1

15 Write a multiple of 7 between 30 and 40. ____

16 What is the smallest number that is a multiple of 2 and 3? ____ 2

17 $4^2 + 6^2 =$ ____ 1

18 Write a **prime number** to make this number sentence true.

20 < _____ < 30

Look at the shaded area on these circles and write the correct letter for each question.

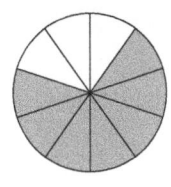 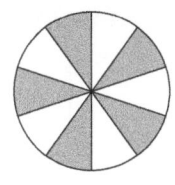 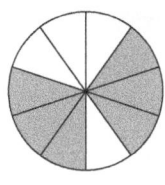 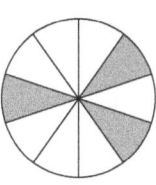

A   B   C   D

19 Which circle has 0.5 shaded? _____

20 Which circle has 70% shaded? _____

21 Which circle has $\frac{3}{5}$ shaded? _____

22 What is $\frac{1}{4}$ of 24? _____

Write the missing numbers in this sequence.

23–24   89   _____   83   _____   77   74

25–26 Write the missing square numbers.

_____   81   64   49   _____

Look at this triangle.

27 What is the name of this triangle? Underline the answer.

isosceles   equilateral
scalene   right-angled

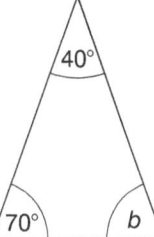

28 Calculate the size of angle *b*. Angle *b* = _____°

29 Circle the net that will make a pyramid when it is folded.

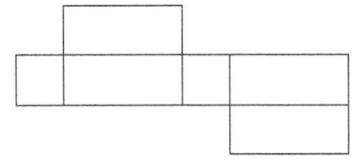   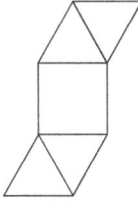   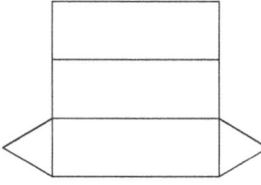

49

30 How many triangular faces are there on a tetrahedron? _____ faces

31 A photo is 12 cm by 5 cm wide. A length of wood is used to make a frame for the perimeter of the photo.

What is the length of the wood for this frame? _____ cm

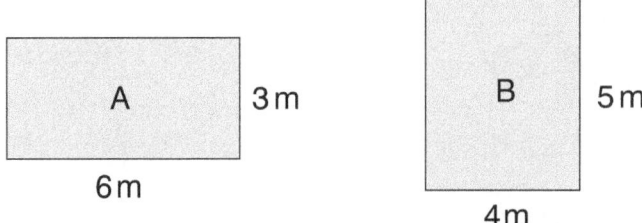

32 Underline the statement that is true.

A has a longer perimeter than B.   B has a longer perimeter than A.

A and B have the same length perimeter.

33 What is the difference in area between rectangles A and B? _____ m²

34 What is the area of a room that is 8 m by 6 m? _____ m²

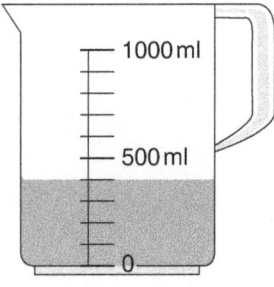
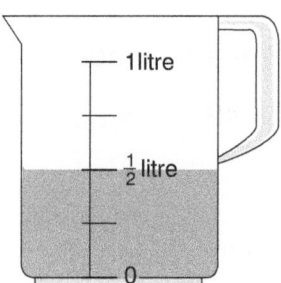

35 What is the difference between the amount of liquid in these two jugs? _____ ml

36 What is the total amount of liquid in these two jugs? _____ ml

37 2 kg + 1500 g = _____ g

38 Belle's dentist appointment was at 11:10 a.m. She arrived 15 minutes early.

What time did Belle arrive at the dentist? _____

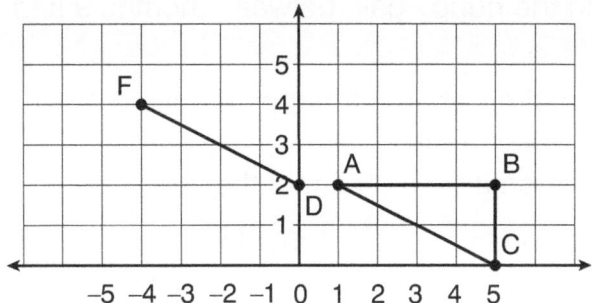

39 Write the coordinates of point C. (____, ____)

40 Write the coordinates of point D. (____, ____)

41 Point E is at (−4, 2). Plot this point and label it.

42 Draw two lines to join D to E and E to F to make a triangle. Underline the word that describes the movement of triangle ABC to the position of triangle DEF.

       reflection   rotation   translation

This graph shows the weight of a puppy each month in its first year of life.

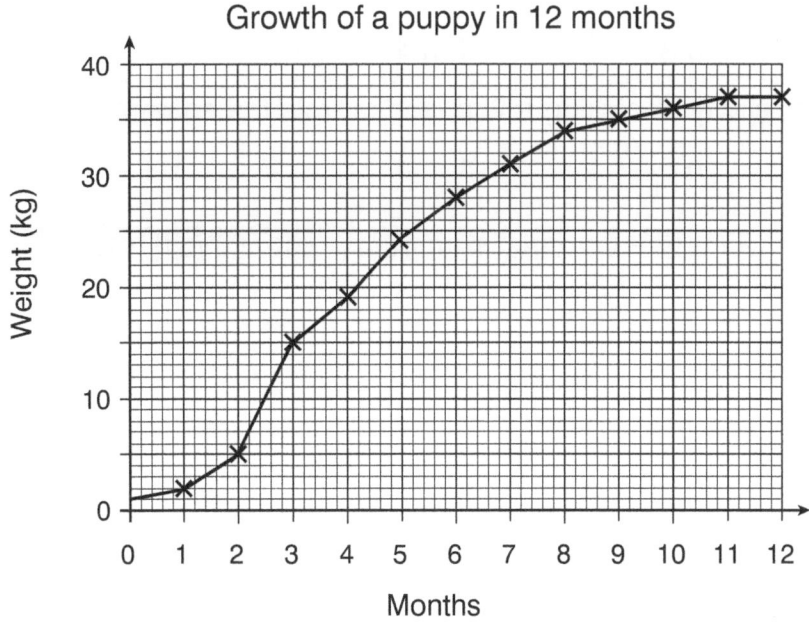

43 How much did the puppy weigh at 1 month old? ____ kg

44 How old was the puppy when it weighed 15 kg? ____ months

45 How much weight did the puppy gain between months 9 and 10?
_____ kg

46 Underline the period of time when the puppy grew the most.

> 0–1 month   1–2 months
>
> 2–3 months   3–4 months

Calculate the median and mean of these lengths.

    12 cm   9 cm   11 cm   8 cm   20 cm

47 Median length =   _____ cm

48 Mean length =   _____ cm

There are four coins in a purse.

49 What is the probability of picking a 5p coin? Circle the answer.

    1 in 2   1 in 3   1 in 4

50 What is the probability of picking a 20p coin? Circle the answer.

    1 in 2   1 in 3   1 in 4

Now go to the Progress Chart to record your score!   Total